WHAT ARE THEY SAYING ABOUT VIRTUE?

What Are They Saying About Virtue?

John W. Crossin, O.S.F.S.

PAULIST PRESS
New York/Mahwah

The Publisher gratefully acknowledges the use of tne following materials:

Excerpts from *Insight and Responsibility* by Erik H. Erikson, W. W. Norton & Company, Inc., copyright © 1964 by Erik H. Erikson are used by permission. The chart "Psycho-social Crises" is reprinted from *The Life Cycle Completed, A Review,* by Erik H. Erikson, by permission of W. W. Norton & Company, Inc., copyright © 1982 by Rikan Enterprises, Ltd.

Library of Congress
Catalog Card Number: 84-62156

ISBN: 0-8091-2674-5

Published by Paulist Press
997 Macarthur Boulevard
Mahwah, N.J. 07430

Printed and bound in the
United States of America

Contents

Preface

In the midst of the tumult and diversity of contemporary theology, a renewed interest in Christian virtue is emerging. This energetic emergence, inchoate as it now appears, promises a vital contribution to moral and spiritual theologies. The purpose of our present study is to show, if only very rapidly and succinctly, the general outline and tenor of the varied theologies of virtue and Christian character. While imperfect, they offer much for future reflection and integration.

The present work has come into being only with the help and encouragement of many people. Prime among these are Dr. William E. May, Dr. John Kinnane and Rev. Thomas Kane, O.P., of Catholic University, who guided me in my doctoral dissertation from which several parts of this study are drawn. Likewise, I owe a great deal to Rev. Joseph Tylenda, S.J., to Rev. Joseph Chorpenning, O.S.F.S., and to Rev. Mr. Robert Del Santo, O.S.F.S., all of whom read this manuscript and offered many helpful suggestions. I am most grateful to Mrs. Marianne Hanton who showed infinite patience in the typing and revising of the text. Finally, I would like to note with gratitude that this work was published with the permission of my Provincial Superior, V. Rev. Richard Reece, O.S.F.S.

Introduction

The question of the birth, growth, and development of Christian character and virtue, which has been a perennial concern of the Christian community, has once again become a focus of attention in contemporary theology and spirituality. The virtue tradition, seemingly comatose a decade or so ago, has recently been showing renewed signs of vitality and strength. Only a few years ago, Jacques Pohier remarked that the word "virtue" in Catholic theology carried a "musty smell of moralizing,"[1] and he called for an account of virtue which would take cognizance of modern psychological insights into the nature of the human person. Now, signs abound of an ongoing renewal of virtue thinking in both Catholic and Protestant circles. Not only has Stanley Hauerwas offered his provocative account of what he calls Christian character in his *Character and the Christian Life,*[2] but a number of important historical studies have indicated the true breadth and depth of virtue thinking in the Christian tradition.[3]

Virtue thinking is also having a discernible renaissance in philosophical circles. Alasdair MacIntyre's book *After Virtue*[4] is having a wide impact among philosophers and many others. In his work MacIntyre argues that the modern person has very largely lost comprehension of morality. Arguments for rival moral claims, while seemingly quite rational, lead back to divergent premises which ultimately rest on personal preferences. Modern moral discourse thus tends to be "emotivist" in nature. The central characters of modern society—the aesthete, the therapist, and the bureaucratic manager—generally embody emotivist modes in their action, if not always explicitly in their thought. MacIntyre traces the contemporary moral impasse to the Enlightenment's rejection of the classical view that the human person has an essential nature and an essential purpose or goal. And "...once the notion of essential human purposes or functions disappears from morality, it begins to appear implausible to treat moral judgments as factual statements."[5]

The solution to the contemporary moral impasse, which shows itself in so many interminable moral and political arguments, lies in a return to the Aristotelian concept of virtue. It is within the context of the virtuous life that rules and the discussion of specific courses of action make sense. It is only by virtuous living that the person attains the fullness of humanity. For Aristotle and for MacIntyre, "...the exercise of the virtues is a necessary and central part of such a life, not a mere preparatory exercise to secure such a life."[6] MacIntyre builds on Aristotle in developing his own distinctive view of human practices and virtues. He moves further in showing that the virtues develop within the unitive story or narrative of a person's entire life. A grasp of narrative tradition and settings is crucial to understanding full human development and flourishing. MacIntyre concludes by advocating small communities as settings for virtuous living in the present age of general moral confusion and fragmentation.

MacIntyre's somewhat surprising embrace of Aristotelian "teleology" and virtue ethics has caused quite a stir in philosophical circles. It has called into question the liberal individualist point of view which moral philosophers have been seeking to justify for the last three centuries. The existence of such a significant debate points to the possible importance of the virtues and virtue thinking for the modern person. If MacIntyre prevails, a major shift in the structure of present-day moral argument, and perhaps even in patterns of living, will ensue.

Our purpose in this volume, however, will not be to examine virtue theory in contemporary philosophy. Rather, we will seek to present an overview of current theological reflection on virtue and Christian character. Theological reflection is not completely separated from current philosophy, but the main thrust and some of the pressing concerns of theology are not those of philosophy. There can be and is fruitful interchange going on between the two fields, but there also are some distinctive paths which theologians will tread alone. Revelation and grace, for instance, impinge on the theologian's reflection in a way which leads to substantial differences between his or her work and that of the philosopher.

Theological reflection on virtue and Christian character is a potentially rich, creative, and integrative field of endeavor. Not only does it embrace philosophy, but it also is broad enough to include moral and spiritual theology, liturgy, and developmental psychology, to name just a few areas of intersection. Moral theology, for instance, might be fruitfully conceived as primarily concerned with the virtues of Christian moral living. In the period prior to the Second Vatican Council (1962-65), Catholic thinking, as exemplified in the manuals of moral theology used to train Catholic seminarians, tended to focus on the rightness or wrongness of specific acts. Likewise, much American Protestant ethics, perhaps under the influence of modern philosophy, tended to concern itself with the evaluation of acts. Recent currents seek to redress this imbalance in Catholic and Protestant theologizing. Catholic theologians of various schools of thought today put much more stress on the person who acts, while Hauerwas' work mentioned above has shown that an ethics of character is consistent with important strains in Protestant ethics (e.g., the work of Calvin, Wesley) and has challenged the prevailing concern with rules and acts. While much work remains to be done, a recognition of the importance of virtue-thinking for moral theologizing seems to be arising.

Concern with the actor rather than just with the act itself points to a crucial link of moral and spiritual theologies through the theology of virtue. Spiritual theology talks about the growth of the Christian in love for God and neighbor. It concerns itself a great deal with the positive side of the Christian life as set out by the spiritual masters. It speaks of the virtues of the spiritual life and how they might be lived out effectively. It recognizes that the Christian is called to grow in love for God and neighbor in many very practical daily ways. In all this, spiritual theology speaks very directly about growth in virtue.

Spiritual theology also speaks very concretely of growth in holiness or sanctification. Traditional Catholic spirituality, for example, spoke of the purgative, illuminative, and unitive ways as stages of spiritual growth. Today there is a great deal of talk about psychological development. The developmental stages of Piaget and Erikson are familiar to many high school and most college students. The studies of adult development by Daniel Levinson[7] and others, which were popularized by Gail Sheehy in her best-sellers *Passages* and *Pathfinders,*[8] have also had a wide impact. The task of spiritual theologians, one which seems to have been eagerly embraced, is that of integrating these, admittedly incomplete, findings into the Christian understanding of spiritual growth. The diversity of the three major contemporary psychological schools—the psychoanalytic, behaviorist, and humanistic—as well as the multitude and variety of information provided, increases the difficulty of this task of integration. But the creative possibilities of such work urge the task forward. Similarly, developmental data is increasingly impacting on the considerations of moral theology. A vibrant theology of virtue, intersecting as it does with moral and spiritual theologies, will also be aware of the natural and cultural developmental thrusts of human growth. This data, too, should have its impact on contemporary virtue theology.

The development of Christian character and virtue occurs not only in the midst of the wider community, but also more particularly within the Church. The community of believers with its Scripture, its tradition, its liturgy, etc., helps and enables the believer to shape his or her own character.[9] Liturgy, for example, molds or at least can mold the perspectives and attitudes of the believer. It can present the moral content of the Christian message. It can help to form Christians as moral agents. The liturgy and the whole of the scriptural narrative nourishes the virtues of the Christian life.[10]

All of the varied elements mentioned so briefly above come together, or at least can come together, in the discussion of Christian virtue. Presently there is a great deal of ferment going on. Theologians are beginning to turn their attention to Christian character, but their work in many cases is incipient or perhaps seminal. In all cases, contemporary virtue theory can be seen to be in a state of evolution. A number of important issues have arisen which need to be dealt with more clearly. For instance, the exact relationship of the individual act to the formation of character needs to be further delineated. The current theological literature tends to emphasize the importance of the character of the person as he or she expresses himself or herself in an individual act. The stress here is very much on the community's role in shaping the person. However, further investigation needs to probe the relation of the individual act to the character of the person. That is, the person forms his or her character or virtue through specific deeds.[11] The deed affects the character, and the character affects the deed. There needs to be a further consideration of this relationship. On this and many other questions, contemporary virtue ethics is still just beginning to come to grips with what is involved and its ramifications. The present-day revival of virtue-thinking is still just beginning and is gradually evolving.

The plan of this small volume is to acquaint the reader with the current state of virtue-thinking. It will offer a survey of some significant current approaches to virtue and Christian character. This survey will not be all inclusive by any means; rather, it hopes to be representative. It will point out the variety of approaches being taken by modern theologians in the United States or by theologians whose works have had a wide impact on thinking in this country.

The work will proceed by offering an exposition of the work of some Catholic thinkers and follow this by an examination of some Protestant thought, especially that of Stanley Hauerwas. After these expositions, it will turn to Erik Erikson's psychosocial theory of the life cycle and point out its influence on several developmental theories of virtue. These will be followed by an investigation of theories of moral development and of faith development advocated by Lawrence Kohlberg and James Fowler, respectively. Finally, the work will conclude with some mention of the problematic elements in contemporary virtue theory and will point to the possibilities of an Augustinian/Salesian approach as a unified approach to Christian virtue.

Before beginning this investigation of the evolving

state of virtue, however, a few words need to be said about the biblical foundations for virtue-thinking. This will provide an important setting for the theological considerations which follow.

Biblical Foundations for the Theology of Virtue

While thinking about virtue and the virtues has been prominent in the history of Christianity, the term virtue is not prominent in the Old or the New Testaments. The Old Testament, while aware of many human virtues, had no single term to express the general idea of virtue. It is only when the Old Testament was translated into Greek that the concept virtue (arete) begins to appear. Here " ..the word indicates divine power (Is 42:8; Zech 6:13; Hab 3:3), but it is also significant of the religious-moral conduct of the pious (Wis 4:1; 5:13; 8:7)."[12] The New Testament is also quite sparing in its use of the term "virtue." The term is only used four times in the entire New Testament (Phil 4:8; 1 Pet 2:9; 2 Pet 1:3; 1:5). Yet exhortations to what would now commonly be called virtues are rather commonplace.[13] A reason sometimes offered for this reticence is that the word may be too anthropocentric and given to delusions of human achievement and merit.[14] The New Testament would more properly stress the saving power of God.

If the word "virtue" is uncommon in the New Testament, the mention of specific virtues and vices is not (e.g., Gal 5:22–23; Rom 1:29–31). The New Testament often contains lists of varied vices and virtues. These show both Jewish and Greek influences. "In the older catalogs the Jewish influence seems to be stronger, whereas in the catalogs of the Pastoral Epistles it is the Greek influence which is dominant."[15] It is the Christian influence, however, which predominates. Virtues are seen as ultimately the effect of the

Holy Spirit and not of human effort. Faith and love are the central virtues which transform those others which come from pagan or Jewish roots.

Similar to the lists of virtues and vices are the lists of duties toward one's neighbor (e.g., Eph 5:22—6:9; Col 3:18—4:1). These, too, are reoriented from a Christian perspective. Some recent investigations point to the influence of Aristotelian political philosophy rather than Stoicism on the construction of these lists.[16] The lists seem to be essentially an attempt to deal with social life from the standpoint of Christian values.

The varied ethical lists and the concrete discussion of various virtues in the Old and New Testaments provide a touchstone and a point of reference for theological discussions of virtues and Christian character. These discussions, of course, generally go far beyond the biblical data. Present discussions of spiritual and religious growth also seek to root themselves in Scripture. James and Evelyn Whitehead, for example, note that sowing and harvesting are frequent scriptural images for growth (e.g., Gen 26:12; 1 Cor 3:6). Human efforts are complemented greatly by God who gives the increase. Similarly, human development is often seen in terms of the architectural metaphor of building or building up (e.g., Mt 7:24–27; 1 Thess 5:11; Eph 4:16). The community is being built up as the body of Christ. Growth is not merely individual, but is also communal. On the negative side, spiritual growth is also against nature. The Christian is grafted onto a cultivated olive tree (Rom 11:24). In development, there is something negative to be overcome by the grace of God. Growth is both natural and contrary to nature.[17]

These few remarks on the scriptural foundations for a theology of virtue bring this introduction to its completion. The summary which we have just given of the breadth of integration, the state of evolution, and the scriptural foundations of this area of theological investigation will serve as a necessary and hopefully useful introduction to the exposition which follows.

1
Virtue in Contemporary Catholic Thought

Reflection on the virtues in Catholicism dates back to the earliest period of the Church. Concern for the virtues is very evident in the later books of the New Testament and in other writings, such as the *Didache,* which date from approximately the same period. The early Church was very much concerned with the actual practice, the living out of the Christian life, rather than with any theoretical consideration of the virtues. Soon, however, efforts were made to relate the Christian conception to the classical Greek understanding of virtues. St. Ambrose, for example, spoke of the four cardinal virtues of prudence, justice, courage, and temperance which were the classical virtues of Plato, Aristotle, and Cicero. St. Augustine, too, spoke of the cardinal virtues and related them to Christian love, seeing these virtues as varied manifestations of love. Down through the centuries, Catholic thinkers have continued to discuss the virtues of Christian living. Various theological syntheses have emerged, the most prominent and influential of which is that of St. Thomas Aquinas. St. Thomas spoke of natural and supernatural virtues in a unique and powerful synthesis of nature and grace. Since the medieval period, Catholic theologians have continued to reflect on the theological virtues of faith, hope, and charity and the moral virtues of Christian life in a variety of ways. The moral manuals used in seminaries before Vatican II, for example, devoted detailed attention to virtues, their definition, and their interrelation. The current flowering of interest in virtues, then, can root itself deeply in the fertile ground of previous reflection.

This chapter will focus on the most recent growth of the Catholic virtue tradition in the work of contemporary Catholic thinkers on virtue. It will examine the contemporary Thomism of Josef Pieper, the existential approach of Romano Guardini, the dynamism of grace of Karl Rahner, the eschatological virtues of Bernard Haring, and the contemporary Catholic emphasis on the virtue of justice. While necessarily summary and selective, this overview hopes to capture both the breadth and depth of current Catholic reflection on virtue and to convey, perhaps more implicitly than explicitly, the excitement inherent in the present revival of interest in virtue. The varied possibilities of the current renewal still remain to be explored.

Contemporary Thomism: Josef Pieper

The vibrancy of the virtue tradition lies in a very important way in reappropriating the old in light of the present situation. Josef Pieper has devoted a long and distinguished academic career to reflecting on the virtues. He has taken the vision of St. Thomas and shown how it is vitally relevant for today. In his best known work, *The Four Cardinal Virtues,*[1] Pieper gives a contemporary understanding of prudence, justice, fortitude, and temperance following the teaching of Aquinas. He shows that these virtues are all intrinsically related and help the human person attain the fullness of his or her nature.

The virtues for Pieper are not a mere gathering together or juxtaposition of character traits, but rather point to the fullness of human being. Humans can never attain to this completion of their being here on earth and so are always "on the way."

> We are "ganz und gar dynamische Wirklichkeit"—and therefore, because we are not yet perfected, we experience in our lives the *ought* of duty.... The virtues picture for us what a person would be if his or her nature were fully realized. This suggests at the outset that no list of virtues can be made from neutral ground, that any depiction of virtues will reflect beliefs about human nature and its possibilities. And, for Pieper at least, no such depiction can be adequate if it ignores our God-relation, if it lacks a vision of human beings as *creatures*.... Virtue is not finally or simply a possession; it is a quest for what can only be received.[2]

The fullness of virtue, then, implies grace and thus is gift. The natural virtues find their completion in that which is beyond and transformative of nature.

In this context, it is possible to consider briefly the moral virtues as Pieper discusses them. Prudence for him is not the small-mindedness or narcissism of some contemporaries, but rather the mold of all the moral virtues. Prudence shapes all human volition and action. It is "reason perfected in the cognition of truth." Here

> "Reason" means...nothing other than "regard for and openness to reality," and "acceptance of reality." And "truth" is to him nothing other than the unveiling and revelation of reality, of both natural and super-natural reality. Reason "perfected in the cognition of truth" is therefore the receptivity of the

human spirit, to which the revelation of reality, both
natural and supernatural reality, has given substance.[3]

This receptivity shows itself in prudent decisions based
both on universal principles and on individual situations
and events. It shows itself in action. Prudence is no mere
theorizing nor is it logical certainty of decision. Prudent
decisions express themselves in actions which seem reasonable, though absolute certainty in such decisions is
often impossible.

To gain the virtue of prudence, a person must be able to
engage in the silent contemplation of reality. True memory,
open-mindedness, and objectivity are called for. Prudence
in decision making often grows in relation to a good and
prudent friend. Such a friend can "stand in one's shoes" and
give advice and direction of high quality.

Prudence, finally, bears a strong relationship to charity. Only the soul which really loves the good can be prudent,
but only the prudent soul can really do the good. Charity
orients the soul to its last end (which is God) and so is said to
be the form of all the moral virtues. Charity affects the core
of even the most common of human actions though it might
not change their outward appearance. Charity molds and
remolds prudence, though it is difficult to say how this
happens in practice because charity is essentially a gift of
God beyond human control.

Beyond this "normal" molding of prudence by charity,
there stands the higher prudence of the saints which holds
as nothing the things of this world. Here God's friends see
reality so deeply that their prudence is transformed.

If prudence is naturally the mold of all the virtues, justice
is the virtue of greatest concern to people today. Justice
involves giving to each person what is his or her due. St.
Thomas speaks of justice as "...a habit *(habitus)* whereby a

man renders to each one his due with constant and perpet-
ual will."[4]

If justice gives to each one his due, then right to what is
due must logically come before justice. Pieper explains that

Man has inalienable rights because he is created a
person by the act of God, that is, an act beyond all
human discussion. In the ultimate analysis, then
something is inalienably due to man because he is
creatura. Moreover, as *creatura,* man has the absolute duty to give another his due.[5]

The human person, however, has no claim on God
because he or she has no right to creation itself as something due.

By definition, justice brings the individual into relationship with another. This justice toward others is realized
especially in external acts. In fact, every external act is
either just or unjust. Such external acts can be evaluated by
objective criteria. Yet for Pieper acts which seem at first
glance to be purely interior, such as the disciplining of
appetites, can involve giving or withholding from a person
what is truly due to him or her. The partner in justice is thus
normally seen to be another individual. However, the
partner can also be the social community or God himself.

Justice is the highest of the three strictly moral virtues.
It is considered as having three basic forms—commutative,
distributive, and legal. These three correspond to the fundamental structures of human community and govern respectively the relationships of individuals to each other, of the
social whole to the individuals, and of the individuals to the
social whole.

Finally, Pieper speaks of the limits of justice. The virtue
of religion, for example, is related to justice but is such that

one's true debt to God can never be repaid. So one tries to pay back whatever is possible. Similarly, he speaks of *pietas,* that virtue of respect for parents and country, and of *observantia,* that inward and outward respect shown to distinguished persons. For human communal life to flourish, mere justice is not sufficient. Rather, these three virtues and a certain friendliness are necessary to a joyful and thriving community life.

The third of the cardinal virtues is fortitude. Fortitude presupposes human vulnerability. The human person is subject to injury and death. All Christian fortitude stands in some way in relation to death. The highest expression of fortitude for the Christian is martyrdom. This willingness to suffer injury and even death is not for any love of suffering for its own sake, but rather to achieve a deeper human wholeness.

Pieper sees fortitude as essentially a secondary virtue. It is not independent, but rather stands in a necessary relationship with prudence and justice. While prudence and justice direct the human person to knowing and doing the good, fortitude and temperance keep the person from moving away from the good.

Fortitude includes a certain human vitality and always works for a just cause. Fortitude knows fear and, in fact, presupposes it, but does not allow such fear to force it to evil or to keep it from doing good. Fortitude has two basic acts, endurance and attack, and of these endurance is more essential. Such endurance involves a strong grasping of and holding on to the good. It is here that patience, a necessary aspect of fortitude, enters. "To be patient means to preserve cheerfulness and serenity in mind in spite of injuries that result from the realization of the good."[6] This is not to say that patience is not energetic, but rather that it excludes sadness. Fortitude also includes that justified anger which can energize the attack on evil. Fortitude and wrath can work together.

The fortitude of the Christian can be distinguished into: (1) the "political" fortitude of everyday life, (2) the "purgatorial" fortitude of purification of soul, and (3) the "mystical" fortitude of the unfolding of God's love and the gifts of the Spirit. Fortitude in all these cases involves letting go of self and abandoning personal anxiety. Supernatural fortitude crowns all natural forms of fortitude and transforms them.

The last of the four cardinal virtues is temperance. Temperance is not mere moderation in food and drink and in anger as common speech today would have it. Temperance is rather the proper disposition of parts into an ordered whole and, secondly, a certain serenity of spirit which flows from this ordering.

Temperance is distinguished from the other cardinal virtues in that it focuses exclusively on the person himself or herself. Prudence embraces all of reality; justice deals with other persons; fortitude invokes self-forgetfulness. But temperance aims at the individual. It concerns the preservation of individual integrity. Intemperance is self-destructive, as the individual selfishly misuses his or her powers. Only if the human powers are actively disciplined and ordered can the person flourish.

The virtue of temperance embraces a number of virtues which rightly order the sensitive powers of the human person.

To sum up: chastity, continence, humility, gentleness, mildness, *studiositas* are modes of realization of the discipline of temperance; unchastity, incontinence, pride, uninhibited wrath, *curiositas* are forms of intemperance.[7]

Each of these virtues and vices are discussed in detail by Pieper. In the course of this discussion, Pieper notes that, while temperance stands behind justice and fortitude in the ordering of the virtues, it comes before them in a certain sense in that it is most often called into practice.

Pieper concludes by saying that the order of temperance brings beauty to the soul. Temperance both liberates and purifies the soul and thus helps it to shine more brightly in God's image.

The discussion of the four cardinal virtues which has just been completed not only makes these virtues more familiar, but also shows the depth and coherence of the Thomistic position. For Pieper, as for St. Thomas, the virtues form a unity.[8] Growth in virtue is a gift that is focused outward and is not an assured possession merely facilitating self-actualization. To think of virtue as a self-possession is to vitiate the Christian virtue of hope.

> The answer to the danger of self-centeredness in the virtuous life seems to be...that (1) we recognize the futility of concern solely for self; and (2) our attempts to cultivate the virtues in our life always be ordered not merely toward self-cultivation, but toward the virtues-as-aid-to-prudent-and-just-activity.[9]

Virtue ultimately focuses outward to others and is no mere self-possession or narcissism.

As this brief summary has attempted to indicate, Josef Pieper offers an illuminating contemporary account of the Thomistic theology of virtue. This synthesis continues to make a major contribution to the ongoing discussion of virtue. Its coherence and clarity make it a touchstone for any thorough discussion of the topic.

The Existentialism of Romano Guardini

In contrast to Pieper's vigorous Thomism, Romano Guardini offers a much less systematic study of virtue from a phenomenological, experiential perspective. He seeks to move his reader from ordinary experience to moral self-realization. For him the concept of virtue is not that "wretchedly deficient character" which has accrued in the course of history, but rather the ability to see in one glance the whole existence of the person.

> Then what does it mean? It means that the motives, the powers, the actions and the being of man are gathered at any given time into a characteristic whole by a definitive moral value, an ethical dominant so to speak.[10]

Virtue embraces then our distinctive attitude to the world. It includes dispositions to both spiritual joy and spiritual suffering. Virtue penetrates the whole of a person's existence, giving life a basic harmony or unity. It is possible, however, that virtue can become compulsive or even rigid. The person must have control even over virtue to become the true image of God.

Virtue ascends toward God or, more precisely, comes down from him. That is, each virtue is a diffraction of the infinitely rich simplicity of God upon human potentiality. But since different individuals have different potentialities, they are related more or less to the various virtues. Hence, there is a kaleidoscope of individual virtues or, perhaps more precisely, of emphasis among the virtues in the lives of individuals.

Guardini's list of virtues is not the classical one, but rather those which seem relevant to the person today. These include truthfulness, acceptance, patience, justice, reverence, and so forth. Each of these virtues is discussed in some detail and in contemporary terms. For example, truthfulness is the first virtue that Guardini discusses. Truthfulness basically means that the person should say what is so and what is in his or her mind to another person who has the right to be so informed. Truthfulness conforms itself to that instinctive human feeling that one should tell the absolute truth. Truthfulness, through repetition, can become a habit which brings to the whole person a certain clarity and firmness. This advent of truth will be accompanied by love. As St. Paul says, we need "to speak the truth in love" (Eph 4:15). Our desire for the truth develops or can develop into the complete truth if two elements are present. The first of these is consideration for the person being addressed and the second is courage when telling the truth becomes difficult. In addition, a person needs a certain understanding of life and its ways. The important core element here is, however, the will to truth. Through it "...a true selfhood comes into being, in the profoundest depths of existence beyond all tension and disturbance."[11]

Truthfulness is the bedrock of human and communal relationships. Without truth, community founders. Without truth, relationships deteriorate. Truthfulness enables two people, who are ultimately mysteries, to come into contact. Ultimately, truthfulness brings a person into contact with God. God himself is Truth. In holding to the truth, we are holding to God.

A second virtue which Guardini discusses is acceptance. This virtue is the presupposition for all effective moral effort. Here he is speaking of "...the acceptance of what is, the acceptance of reality, your own and that of the people around you, and of the time in which you live."[12] This is not a weak submissiveness, but a clear-eyed view of the truth upon which a person can build by decisive action. Such is needed because human desires often exceed human being. This clear tension is often evident in human living.

Acceptance means first of all that a person must accept himself or herself. Each person is an individual with a definite character, temperament, possibilities and limitations. Each person has both strengths and weaknesses. Thus, each must learn to accept the self as is and build on the available material. This is no justification for avoiding attempts to improve, but rather a realistic assessment of personal existence.

Moving beyond self and individual strengths and weaknesses, a person must learn to accept the situation and circumstances of life. While many things can change, others are set early in life. One's destiny is a determination of outer events and inner character. One's destiny relates both to inner dispositions and to the fortunes and misfortunes of life itself. One's destiny is ultimately in the hands of Divine Providence and so can be accepted. In this light, misfortunes which cannot be avoided can not only be endured, but even be accepted in their bitterness.

Finally, acceptance "...of self means that I simply consent to be."[13] When life is oppressive and wearying, one chooses to accept and to be. Such acceptance rests on the perception that life comes from God and God is well-disposed toward us. In Christ, God approaches humanity. Through faith in God and God's salvific work in Christ, we can come to a comprehension, mastery, and ultimate acceptance of personal being.

It is easy to see from these two examples of virtue the

great difference between Pieper and Guardini. Different philosophical starting points and concerns lead to quite varying discussions and lists of virtues. Here the variety of the Catholic virtue tradition begins to come clearly into focus. This variety will be even more in evidence as we continue.

Karl Rahner: The Dynamism of Grace

While Guardini represents current Catholic concern for the existential and the concrete, Karl Rahner, considered by many today to have been the Catholic Church's leading contemporary theologian, represents the concern for the efficacy of grace in the existential situation. Rahner's thinking on the virtues is a part of his wider systematic reflection on the whole of Catholic theology. He is the prime representative of the school of theological thought known as transcendental Thomism. For him, human life is especially graced by God both implicitly and explicitly.[14] Virtue, generally speaking, is a fully developed capacity of the human soul and, more particularly, is "the power to realize the moral good" with joy and perseverance even in the face of obstacles. The virtues which God infuses into the human heart are the dynamism of sanctifying grace. These virtues are closely related to the grace of justification and "...are only distinguished from the grace which divinizes man's very being as its dynamic extension into his faculties...."[15]

For Rahner, the supernatural virtues orient the natural virtues toward God. But since, in the presently existing real order of salvation, the natural virtues already have a supernatural goal and the supernatural virtues are lived out in the harsh reality of daily life, the distinction between natural and supernatural virtues is not of great importance. Faith, hope and charity are, as the Council of Trent teaches, infused into the soul with the grace of justification. The fact that these virtues orient persons so strongly to God, however, makes the question of infused moral virtues more a question of terminology than anything else.

The three theological virtues develop historically and come to their fullness in love. Each virtue can be seen as a "moment" in the procession toward charity and only in this manner can we speak of the separateness of the virtues. Faith is the beginning of this process of development. It is the recognition of and commitment to the goal. It is a personal decision. Out of the concrete experience of human existence, a person can come to experience Christianity as being the real truth and wholeness of life. The logic here is that of the virtue of faith. Human experience at its deepest level disposes a person toward faith.

The second of the theological virtues, hope, is that virtue which draws the person out of self. It provides a certain dynamism to the other theological virtues. It propels the soul outward into a future which cannot be seen. In traditional Scholastic theology, hope often seemed to be reduced to a passing mode of faith and love. Rahner argues that hope, which, as St. Paul says, will remain forever, is much more important. Hope moves the person out from self.

Hence "hope" does not, in this most ultimate sense, express a modality of faith and love so long as these are at the provisional stage. On the contrary, it is a process of constantly eliminating the provisional in order to make room for the radical and pure uncontrollability of God. It is the continuous process of destroying that which appears, in order that the absolute and ultimate truth may be the intelligible as comprehended, and love may be that which is brought about by our love.[16]

Hope unifies the faith and love of the believer. This hope, too, does not pass away in eternal life. Rather, since the Beatific Vision is not a matter of comprehension of God, but proximity to the Absolute Mystery who is God, the dynamism of hope with its self-emptying is still called for. Thus, hope endures forever.

Hope, besides making room for the uncontrollability of God, also is that virtue which actually convinces the believer that God's grace is effective for him or her individually. Rahner believes that the theoretical awareness of God's promises of salvation which faith provides is not sufficient to ground the conviction that this saving grace is operative in the life of the believer. Such conviction is provided in the individual's life by hope.

Finally, hope is the basis of a revolutionary attitude by Christians toward the world. That is, hope enables the person to see the structures of secular life as provisional. Hope summons the Christian to decide again and again between defense of the present and movement into the unforseeable future. Hope provides a dynamism not only to the Christian's personal life, but to that from which it cannot be separated, life in society.[17]

The key and central virtue for Rahner is love. All other virtues are "moments" of this most important virtue. Love embraces all of human experience. It includes all of the person as he or she is drawn out of self into the mystery of God. Thus, it is more capable of being described than defined. Love includes both benevolent love and concupiscent love. These are not in mutual conflict. "They are aspects of the same love, which are based on the transcendence of the subject which is capable of affirming and willing the other."[18] This position varies with the emphasis of traditional theology which stresses the opposition of the two loves. For Rahner, the two go together. He also holds that human *eros* is the deep potentiality and longing in the person (obediential potency) for divine *agape*. Here he takes a position which gives a more positive view of the human bodily sexual dynamism than earlier manuals of Catholic theology did.

Rahner continually stresses that the love of God and of neighbor go together. Human love for God is essentially a response to God's love, God's *agape* toward humanity which is God's self-communication. This self-communication makes God the center of creation and of human historicity. This love of God for humanity, while manifested in deeds of love and obscured by the depths of human suffering, remains primarily a mystery to which mankind seeks to respond in love. This response both in love for God and for neighbor most fittingly takes place in the community of the Church.[19]

Our encounter with our neighbor is for Rahner the most important act of human existence. He affirms that "the act by which the neighbor is loved *is* really the primal (though still non-explicit) act by which God is loved."[20] That is, the love of neighbor is not a condition, effect, or fruit of the love of God, but really is itself an act of love of God. Love of God and love of neighbor are one. Rahner believes that many would question him on this position. He goes even further in holding that:

> Whenever man in full and free self-disposition performs a positive moral act, in the actual order of salvation the act is also a positive supernatural salvific act. This is so even if its *a posteriori* object and express motive do not obviously stem from the revealed word of God, but are in this sense "natural." For, by his general salvific will, God offers

divinizing grace to each man and elevates super-
naturally his positive moral acts.[21]

The person in such an act of love can actualize his or
her whole being. That the person would be performing a
religious act and is consciously aware of such remains
secondary. In engaging oneself fully in a positive moral act,
an individual comes quite truly into the order of salvation.

In Rahnerian thought, love for God and love for neighbor are intrinsically related.[22] Grace is dominant and love is
the central virtue. The theological virtues are in the fore-
ground while the natural moral virtues appear truly graced
in this present era of salvation. Rahner offers, then, a systematic view of the virtues which differs quite significantly
from those of Pieper and Guardini discussed above. While
existential like Guardini, Rahner is much more systematic;
while systematic like Pieper, Rahner's stress on the perva-
siveness of grace gives a quite different perspective on and
unity to the virtues.

The Eschatological Virtues of Bernard Haring

Another different and interesting approach to the
virtues and to the virtuous life is offered by the distinguished German moral theologian, Bernard Haring. In his
three volume work, *Free and Faithful in Christ,* Haring offers
a theological synthesis which is based very much on Scripture and which shows the strong influence of spiritual theology. Haring's work is abreast of much contemporary
theology and of the data of the social sciences. He combines
these elements in a broad synthesis which stresses the
complementarity of freedom and faithfulness in creative
and responsible Christian living.

Haring approaches the Christian virtues in light of the theology of the fundamental option. This theology looks at the traditional concept of the ultimate end of the human person in a way which is coherent with the insights of contemporary psychology (e.g., Erik Erikson's concept of identity). The fundamental option is a basic intention or orientation of a person's whole life toward or away from God. It thus embraces more than a single act. "The least we can say here is that a fundamental option is the activation of a deep knowledge of self and of basic freedom by which a person commits himself."[23] This option is not activated in relation to a mere idea, but rather in relation to a person, an Other, who is good. This ethics is an ethics of the heart, an ethics of response to the Other, who is God.

In this context, virtues are part of the development of the fully human person. They involve a person's free choice of positive values, especially those related to other human persons. Virtues are conceived of "...as specific attitudes in response to particular spheres of values. These virtues manifest and promote wholeness and salvation to the extent that they are rooted in the fundamental option of faith."[24] Faith is the grateful acceptance of God's truth and love with one's whole being. It is a commitment to God who is truly good and loving. Christian life is living out this basic commitment in freedom and fidelity.[25] Essential parts of this faith are the traditional theological virtues of hope and love. In particular, love has been seen classically as the "form of all the virtues." Love, for Haring, can be seen in even greater depth if it is examined in light of the fundamental option and the integration of faith and life. One cannot truly be a loving person without knowledge of the virtues, while the virtues and their corresponding spheres of values fit into the overall order of love, as was insisted by St. Augustine.[26] The theological and moral virtues, then, are closely linked.

The virtues for Haring are very much linked with one's fundamental option and intentions. As these penetrate the desires, intuitions, and imagination of the individual, they become those fundamental attitudes of responsiveness to value which are called virtues. It is important to note, however, that these virtues are at root responses in faith to God and not the limited attempts at self-fulfillment or self-realization common to the Stoics and some contemporaries.[27] Virtues are not closed in on self, but rather eschatological in focus. Virtues are gifts of the Spirit for which one renders thanks.

Haring's distinctive contribution in discussing the virtues is his emphasis on the eschatological virtues. He believes that the traditional four cardinal virtues are not characteristic of biblical ethics. Rather, Scripture stresses eschatological virtues. Haring discusses four of these which he labels gratitude-humility, hope, vigilance, serenity and joy.

The two basic attitudes of gratitude and humility are inseparable in Christian life. In seeing God from whom all good things come, the soul gives praise to God for his love and begins to share that love with others. The humility of the Christian shares in the humility of Christ and arises from life in Christ. "Christ's humility does not spring from baseness or inferiority, but flows from the heights above, from the inner wealth and freedom of God's love for us."[28] Humility, then, is nourished in gratitude for the great things God has done for us through Christ his Son. Humility is not focused on personal sinfulness, but rather on God's goodness and mercy. Humility is ultimately a gift of the Spirit which liberates the Christian. While pride essentially disorients the soul and leads to emptiness, humility liberates the soul and exalts it. Through gratitude and humility the person can gradually come to exhibit those attitudes which are expressive of the right fundamental option.

While gratitude and humility remember the great things the Lord has done, hope looks to the future. "Hope give us clear orientation and purpose as co-actors in the on-going creation and redemption. It turns our eyes to the absolute and abiding future in God and makes us clear-sighted about the proximate steps to take."[29] Hope is realistic in uniting the person with Christ. It provides continuity to the fundamental option while being open to change and conversion. Hope remains faithful despite the ups and downs of life. In hope, the Christian is united with others who share this hope and work together for a better future.

If hope looks to the future and gratitude-humility to the past, vigilance focuses on the present moment. The vigilant person reads the "signs of the times" and seeks to discover present opportunities for following the Lord. These are discovered in light of the past and of the future, especially in light of the great events of salvation history. Vigilance also gives attention to the little things of everyday life. It can see the hand of the Lord even in temporary setbacks and suffering. Vigilance enables the person to discern the appropriate thing to do in the present situation and to use the daily events of life to grow in the image of Christ.

As the person grows in the eschatological virtues, his or her fundamental option enters more fully into the Paschal Mystery. This growth is characterized by a certain serenity and joy which is the gift of the Spirit. These virtues keep the individual from any useless worry, anxiety, fear, or scrupulousness. The peace and reconciliation which the Spirit brings strengthen the person to recommit himself or herself to the work of salvation here on earth.

Haring's discussion of the eschatological virtues emphasizes the work of the Spirit in guiding Christian life and growth. He centers on the Scriptures as providing an understanding of the most important virtues for Christian living. By doing so, he highlights another dimension of the richness of the Catholic virtue tradition. This focus on Scripture and on the work of the Spirit provides a balance to any tendency for discussion of the virtues to become too one-sidedly philosophical. Haring emphasizes that it is truly Christian virtue which is under discussion.

The Contemporary Emphasis on Justice

After these brief considerations of the work of several Catholic authors on virtue, it is important to examine briefly the significant and burgeoning reflections on justice in recent Catholic thinking. The Second Vatican Council manifested the Church's ongoing concern for justice issues. This concern continues to be shown in a variety of official statements offered by recent Popes and by various national conferences of bishops.[30] In fact, the second Synod of Bishops meeting in Rome in 1971 affirmed that "Action on behalf of justice and participation in the transformation of the world fully appear to us as a constitutive dimension of the preaching of the Gospel...."[31] There has been some debate since that time as to exactly what the word "constitutive" meant to the fathers who were members of the Synod. We might agree with Charles M. Murphy in his contention that:

> The heart of the ambiguity about the meaning of constitutive, therefore, seems to reside in differing conceptions of what kind of justice is being referred to. If justice is conceived exclusively on the plane of the natural, human virtue of justice as explained in classical philosophical treatises, then such justice can only be conceived as an integral but nonessential part of the preaching of the Gospel. But if justice is conceived in the biblical sense of God's liberating

action which demands a necessary human response
—a concept of justice which is far closer to agape than
to justice in the classical philosophical sense—then
justice must be defined as of the essence of the Gospel
itself. The later sense seems to reflect better the men-
tality of more recent Christian social doctrine.[32]

The exact meaning of the bishops is really a matter of
ongoing theological reflection. But the intent and direction is
quite clear. Justice is intimately linked with the Gospel
message of Christianity. Love of God and love of neighbor
are intrinsically connected with doing justice to those in
society. This emphasis on justice reflects the Gospel's concern with the poor and those who are outcasts and despised.
One sees, then, in the wide ranging thought of Catholic
theology at the present time an overriding concern for justice and the relationship of this virtue to the Christian obligation of loving.

Various contemporary Catholic authors link justice and
love and present the intrinsic connection of these virtues.[33]
This concern for a loving justice is not to be ethereal or
other-worldly. It is, rather, to express itself in concrete
actions which assure justice for those who are oppressed
and outcast. This often leads Catholic writers to a critical
analysis of the economic system in the United States. The
American view rising from a capitalistic society and econ-
omy stands in some contrast to the biblical view of justice
and its concern for the poor and those who are outcast.
While there is some disagreement on these issues in
Catholic circles, the major thrust toward a concern for justice remains intact and is growing. There is a continued
interest in the common good in the United States and what
achieving this common good will entail. Certainly one intrinsic element of achieving the common good is pursuing
justice for all, or at least justice as far as it can be obtained

in the present concrete situation of the ethos of American life. As one author notes, "Justice...is not one more virtue among the many. It is the foundation of civilized human life. It is the primal articulation of the foundational moral experience of the value of life and its environment."[34]

In this context, it is important to note an ongoing concern with what is sometimes referred to as "horizontalism." This refers to the danger of seeing work for justice as a purely human effort rather than as a project undertaken only with the help of God. It is not a matter of "...trying to build the kingdom of God on earth with our own good works, or of trying to make the poor rich. It is a matter of loving as Christ loved—and as God commands."[35] Thus, ultimately one is not attempting a merely human project but a project founded on the love of God and aided, sustained and fulfilled in grace. Christian concern for the poor is rooted deeply in spiritual values.

No discussion of justice is complete without some mention of the contemporary theology of liberation. In his classic work, *A Theology of Liberation,*[36] Gustavo Gutierrez enunciates a comprehensive view of liberation from a Latin American perspective. This liberation is rooted in the scriptural teaching of justice and reflects the experience of those in the Latin American situation. This liberation, as Gutierrez notes in his later work, is centered on Christ. It is beyond "...any suggestion that the world's salvation depends on our efforts. It is precisely the gratuitous quality of God's love, revealed in Jesus, that sets us free to work in the service of God's Kingdom."[37] Certain themes of Latin American liberation theology have been transposed into the different cultural context of the United States, and this transposition leads to a variety of thinking by American Catholic authors. These authors see a need for liberation and justice in the economic and political circumstances of the United States.

Their movement, however, seems to be of an initial nature, though perhaps it will have a wide impact.[38]

These few reflections on the virtue of justice in no way indicate the depth of concern for this virtue in contemporary writing. They serve merely to point to a virtue on which many volumes have been written. Catholic thinking these days is deeply concerned with the virtue of justice. This extends from papal statements, through the declarations of the synods, to the work of contemporary liberationists and of others who are concerned with justice. There is a common agreement that the Gospel imperative leads the Christian to concern for those who are weak and outcast in society. There is some disagreement as to the exact role the Christian and the Church should play in helping those who are in need, but the basic thrust and the message seems clear to all. This is an area of burgeoning development with the potential for immense impact. It is in this area that the theory of justice needs to continue to be explored and the principles of justice further elaborated and delineated. This is an ongoing work which will continue in a vigorous way for years to come.

The purpose of this chapter was to give an overview of the vibrancy and diversity of the virtue tradition in Catholicism. This overview is in no way exhaustive, but it does reflect the state of the question and the vigorous concern expressed by contemporary authors in Christian virtues. We turn now to the substantial and influential contributions of certain Protestant authors to the theology of Christian character and virtue.

2
Christian Character in Contemporary Protestant Ethics

Our initial investigations have indicated the richness and complexity of Catholic reflection on Christian virtue. The point of the present chapter, and the implication of subsequent ones, will be that Protestant ethics too is alive to thinking about virtue and Christian character. While their thought can only be briefly surveyed, the substantial contribution of these authors is obvious and most significant in the current discussion.

One writer of particular present-day significance is the German theologian Jurgen Moltmann. His widely regarded *Theology of Hope*[1] and his subsequent critical theological works provide a provocative attempt to bring together biblical revelation and the present human situation.[2] Moltmann's theologizing has a major thrust toward systematic and dogmatic theology which takes it well beyond the limits and concerns of our present investigation. Yet his emphasis on an eschatological theology of hope which speaks to human suffering and calls for a political theology which seeks human liberation resonates well with the concern for justice we have mentioned previously.

Moltmann shows great awareness of suffering in the world. His theology speaks to this suffering in his reflections on hope. His theology "... is not a theology *about* hope, but a theology growing *out of* hope in God. The basis for this hope does not lie in the ups and downs of the moods of the time, but in the promise of the coming God."[3] This theology is strongly rooted in Scripture. Its eschatological focus seeks to bring "a 'warm stream' of hope"[4] to all the articles of faith. Hope opens up the person and, in a real sense, is the most important constituent of human life. "The living source of hope lies in a future from which new time, new potentiality and new freedom continually advance to meet us. We find this future in Jesus Christ; he is our future—he is our hope."[5]

This hope is grounded in both the death and resurrection of Christ. As M. Douglas Meeks has noted:

> The resurrection creates a qualitatively new future in which the present antagonistic conditions of men will be radically transformed. The cross shows the real presence of God's power in his suffering from and contradiction of those forces which make human life inhuman.[6]

In Christ, human suffering and death have been definitively overcome. Yet Moltmann's focus is not solely on Christ. His developed thinking includes a profound investigation of the Trinity. This Trinitarian theology of the cross, however, leads inevitably to a political theology, "...for in the cross God identified himself with the politically powerless and poured out the Spirit which exalts the weak to confound the strong."[7]

Thus Moltmann stresses human liberation from oppression and suffering. Attempts in this direction must obviously take into account what is possible at the present moment but also must be self-critical and willing to speak out. This may very well bring one into conflict with the world, but this truly is the price one must pay as a disciple. There is a present need for an exodus from those structures which sustain oppression and suffering to those more in tune with human freedom and open to new and creative possibilities for the future. Moltmann's theology of hope calls for a radical engagement in this world.

Moltmann's engaging theology offers a profound reflection on Christian hope. It approaches all of theology from this vital perspective. In so doing, Moltmann exceeds the bounds of our present study, but perhaps indicates the latent possibilities in considering Christian virtues.

Christian Character and Stanley Hauerwas

Another very significant Protestant thinker who has reflected deeply on Christian virtue is the Methodist theologian Stanley Hauerwas. His work on Christian character and narrative is having a sizable impact on contemporary Christian ethics. Hauerwas' imaginative approach to Christian life and action offers a different point of view on present-day ethical concerns.

The roots of Hauerwas' early work seem to lie in the thought of the prominent Christian ethicist James Gustafson. Gustafson has expressed a number of ideas which have been further explicated by other thinkers and, in particular, by his student Hauerwas. A brief exposition of some of Gustafson's central insights will provide a context for understanding the more elaborate reflections on Christian character offered by Hauerwas.

Gustafson contends in *Christ and the Moral Life*[8] that Christian life ought to be characterized by a certain orientation toward the world. This is not to say that every believer has the same perspective, but rather that there is a certain similarity of orientation in that all are committed to Christ. Within this general orientation certain characteristic moral dispositions arise. These are persistent tendencies to act in a certain way and would be called "habits" in the standard Roman Catholic terminology. The distinction between perspective and disposition is that

> Dispositions refer to the self's attitudes, its somewhat stable readiness to speak and to act in particular ways. Perspective and posture refer more to the fundamental points of orientation that are governed by convictions that one has about crucial matters.[9]

He goes on to distinguish disposition from intention. Intention would be much more self-conscious and involve more rational specification. Perspectives, dispositions, and intentions, however, are not isolated but interrelated and embrace more than mere reasonableness.

> To discuss the formation and function of moral intentions in the Christian life makes it sound more objectively rational than it is or even ought to be. The self finds its identity in part by the consistency of its intentions, and the formed identity of the self is expressed in its intentions. This identity, or posture, of the self is the effect of commitments and loyalties that are affective as well as intellectual, that are personal as well as public.[10]

In further elaborating his ideas, Gustafson points out that there are and can be varied Christian styles of life. Judgments as to whether certain styles of life are Christian need to be exercised with caution. In speaking of a Christian style of life

We are speaking qualitatively, both about a pattern
of life that we could develop in normative descriptions, and about the intensity and seriousness with
which that style might be manifest in the intentions,
attitudes and behavior of Christians. We cannot
assess the behavior of Christians, or other attitudes
and intentions, and give a descriptive generaliza-
tion about a style of life that *thereby* becomes
normative.[11]

Christ, of course, is the ultimate model and norm in relation
to which all Christian life-styles can be evaluated.[12]

Stanley Hauerwas, in his initial work with Gustafson,
and in his subsequent writings, has clearly gone far beyond
the general categories just mentioned. In his first major
work, *Character and the Christian Life,* Hauerwas attempted
to rethink Protestant theological ethics from the point of
view of the virtue tradition. In this effort Hauerwas gives
over a whole chapter of his book to analyzing Aristotle's and
Thomas Aquinas' work as a foundation for his ethics of
character. He contends that "Their thought, in spite of
obvious difficulties and ambiguities, continues to be the
most adequate systematic account of the nature of character in the history of ethics."[13] However, he does not rest
content with Aquinas and Aristotle.

Aristotle and Aquinas do not provide a completely
satisfying account of the idea of character, as they
leave many questions ambiguous or unanswered
...This is partly because they simply were not trying to develop a theory of character as such.
Moreover, they assumed certain distinctions, such

as that between movement and activity, as self-evident that require defense.[14]

Hauerwas uses contemporary philosophy to deal with unanswered questions and to build a theory of Christian character. In other writings, Hauerwas has expanded his ideas and further elaborated his conception of Christian living.

Hauerwas' work on vision, narrative, and Christian character has contributed a provocative and interesting chapter to recent discussions of virtue. Hauerwas contends that discussions of Christian morality have focused too much on personal choice, on rationality, and on objectivity. Greater focus needs to be concentrated on the agent and, as Hauerwas emphasized in his early writing on the agent's vision, "The moral life...is more than thinking clearly and making rational choices. It is a way of seeing the world."[15] The Christian has a certain way of seeing and attending to the world. The emphasis on this theological viewpoint falls on everyday activity in which one works at being human. However, "...truthful vision...does not come without discipline. The self must be transformed if we are to attend honestly to how we are to live justly in a contingent world."[16]

The Christian vision is related to the character of the Christian,[17] a notion which Hauerwas develops at great length and on which he seeks to reformulate traditional Protestant theological ethics. This attempt at reformulation has helped create a strong debate in Protestant ethical circles where the ethics of duty has predominated with its emphasis on rationality and moral cases.[18] Hauerwas, while developing his theory from theological and philosophical viewpoints, also seeks to show a positive relationship between his view of Christian character and the ideas on sanctification advanced by Calvin, Wesley and, to a lesser extent, Jonathan Edwards.

For Hauerwas, character is different from possessing individual virtues.

> The idea of character, however, not only denotes a more general orientation than the virtues, but having character is a more basic moral determination of the self. The various virtues receive their particular form through the agent's character.[19]

To speak more precisely, by "character" Hauerwas means "...the qualification of man's self-agency through his beliefs, intentions, and actions, by which a man acquires a moral history befitting his nature as a self-determining being."[20] In stressing character, he emphasizes personal self-determination. A person's actions help determine who he or she is and who he or she will be.[21] In them one can affirm or deny previous self-determinations. People are not merely formed by environmental or psychological factors, but form themselves.

> Man is at the mercy of external forces only if he allows himself to be, for man is not just acted upon but agent. To be a man is to be an autonomous center of activity and the source of one's own determinations; all he knows, all he wills, all he does issues from that very act by which he is.[22]

There is no necessity to posit an internal or external cause of activity. A person simply has the power to act because he or she is human: "We have the power of efficient causation through our capacity to intentionally form our action."[23]

Character, for Hauerwas, affects what a person does

more than rules or more than analyses of situations. Character can and should grow progressively into conformity with Christ.

A third major concomitant to Hauerwas' ideas on vision and character is what he refers to as "narrative" or "story." In fact, narrative and character seem to be the central elements in his most recent reflections. Narrative enables Hauerwas "... to spell out the substantive content of character,"[24] and such narratives are particularly appropriate to those areas "... of our lives that admit of no further explanations—e.g., God, the world, and the self."[25] The concept of narrative enables Hauerwas to pull together the various themes in his theologizing.[26] While he does not believe that story can account for all of theology, Hauerwas does hold that narrative is uniquely suited to the theologian's task. The term "story" is hard to define precisely. "A story... is a narrative account that binds events and agents together in an intelligible pattern."[27] Human action is intentional and historical and, thus, a person needs stories in order to catch the connections between particular, contingent events. Stories affect how we see the world and give a coherence to the jumbled particularities of our lives.

> What is required for our moral behavior to contribute to a coherent sense of the self is neither a single moral principle nor a harmony of the virtues, but...the formation of character by a narrative that provides a sufficiently truthful account of our existence.[28]

Rules and principles take their meaning from the narrative context in which they are embedded. So, too, individual virtues and moral character are embedded in and affected by the ongoing story of an individual's life and the stories which he or she chooses to make his or her own. Conversely, "Our character is constituted by the rules, metaphors, and stories that are combined to give a design or unity to the variety of things we must and must not do in our lives."[29]

The Christian community is the repository for and continual proclaimer of those stories, both biblical and non-biblical (e.g., Augustine's *Confessions*), which make the Christian message come alive for the average person. Community is essential to the formation of Christian character. What is crucial, Hauerwas contends, "... is not that we find some way to free ourselves from such stories or community, but that the story which grasps us through our community is true. And at least one indication of the truthfulness of a community's story is how it forces me to live in it in a manner that gives me the skill to take responsibility for my character."[30]

Recently, Hauerwas' thought has been subject to some systematic analysis and review. Thomas Ogletree finds Hauerwas' writing provocative in its bold, experimental quality.[31] He sees Hauerwas' thought as basically theological in nature with borrowing of selected philosophical categories from analytic philosophy. His philosophical position, then, tends to be somewhat eclectic. The key to Hauerwas' work is that he is calling for a complete re-evaluation of one's normative ethical frame of reference. Ogletree believes that Hauerwas, after his bold ventures, now needs to give some more systematic reflection to his proposed paradigm shift in Christian ethical thinking.

Gene Outka in his review of Hauerwas' work is positive but also raises questions. He believes that Hauerwas needs to define more precisely the relationship between the agent "I" and the social "me," between agency and sociality. Furthermore, he says:

> What I find perplexing is that Hauerwas commands
> such an ethics of vision without asking whether this
> calls for any modification in his account of charac-
> ter, or any lessening of his own normative commit-
> ment to self-determination as such.[32]

Hauerwas has recently reflected on Outka's observations. He contends that freedom derives from having a well-
developed character. That is, in traditional terms, the truly
free person is one who is truly good. For him "... agency but
names our ability to inhabit our character."[33] Furthermore, I
am not primarily an agent because I can make things
happen but because I can take things that happen whether
by my decision or not and fit them into my story. To speak of
agency, then, is to speak of narrative. "There is no contra-
diction between claims of agency and our sociality, since
the extent and power of any agency depends exactly on the
adequacy of the descriptions we learn from our communities."[34] Our character is molded in our relationships to others in the community, and this makes all the difference in
our capacity to be moral agents.

Hauerwas' stress on the distinctiveness of the Christian
story, and hence of Christian ethics, raises questions as to
dialogue with those who are not believers. Are there no
common grounds for dialogue, as in Catholic natural law
thinking, with non-believers? And, further, are there no
intrinsic grounds for considering some practices morally
objectionable (e.g., slavery) no matter what one's particular
narrative?[35]

Furthermore, what is the specific role for moral argument and justification in Hauerwas' theory? That is, for
Hauerwas, the scriptural stories, for example, help to form

the moral character of the Christian. He stresses this formative role. Yet, as James Childress notes,[36] there is more to Scripture than this. Certainly the stories of Scripture are formative, but the Scriptures also contain many types of materials, and principles and rules should not be overlooked. As Richard McCormick asks, "How do the biblical narratives as formative relate to justification in moral discourse?"[37] Or, more generally, are not moral principles and rules necessary to determine what to do in a specific situation even if one is a virtuous person?[38] Legitimate questions such as these point to areas of potential development in Hauerwas' work.

The highly original and provocative work which Hauerwas presents has contributed greatly to the current interest in the ethics of virtue. His work is still evolving and, hopefully, will come to a clearer resolution of the issues raised here. His emphasis on Christian character provides a needed balance to the preoccupation of both Catholic and Protestant ethicists with individual acts.

Further Elaboration on Christian Character

Some interesting elaborations and further reflections on Christian character are offered by Craig Dykstra in his recent book, *Vision and Character*.[39] Dykstra distinguished two basic ways of conceptualizing the moral life. He entitled them "judicial ethics" and "visional ethics." He contends that judicial ethics has been prominent recently, particularly in the work of Lawrence Kohlberg.[40] Dykstra elaborates on what he considers to be Kohlberg's three central themes and shows why he believes that these are false. Dykstra contends that our decisions and choices root themselves not in rules, principles and formal operations, but rather in our vision of reality. He believes that what Kohlberg has discovered can "... be called the stages in the development of social reasoning. By social reasoning I mean the ability to adjudicate explicit claims in situations of social conflict."[41]

Dykstra advocates a visional ethics which has many similarities to the work of Hauerwas. He believes that our vision is one of a world which is shot through with mystery. God confronts us as mystery and we, too, encounter one another as mysteries. That is, people are mysterious and, thus, we cannot completely understand them, just as we cannot completely capture or fix or define the mystery of God. Dykstra believes that the Christian vision goes far beyond the justice which Kohlberg advocates. He says:

> These notions...turn all our natural values topsy-turvy. There is no justice in the sense of equal rights in the cross; yet we are called to bear it. There is no happiness as we ordinarily understand it in accepting suffering about which we can do nothing; yet we are called to remain in it. There is no utility in trusting an ultimate goodness we cannot see or comprehend; yet we are called to do so. But the promise is that in doing these things, we will encounter the world as it is in a way that we could not conceive on our own, and cannot conceive so long as we turn from or reduce these mysteries to something we can handle.[42]

Thus, the person of vision encounters mystery. The emotions, evaluations, predispositions, prejudices, and so on, of the person are truly brought to bear in attending to the world. This attention is most significant for the moral life and depends and interrelates very much to the person who is attending. All this is not to say that vision is removed from reason or rationality. Reason comes strongly to bear, but reason here is not the reasoning embodied in propositions, but rather the common sensical reason which manifests itself in a good story. Stories then, or narratives, are essential to conceiving of the moral life. These stories are, of course, nourished in the Christian community. Communities have character and they in their own way help to shape the character of their members. People within communities relate to the mystery of their fellow members and in communicating help one another to develop.

As with Hauerwas, Dykstra's main emphasis falls on the character and the narrative of the person and not on individual action. Action flows from the vision of the person. "For visional ethics, action follows vision; and vision depends on character—a person thinking, reasoning, believing, feeling, willing, and acting as a whole. In this context, the place of choices, decisions, and actions is a different one."[43] That is, actions grow not so much from universal principles but from the character or narrative or vision of the person within community. Dykstra goes on to note that, while juridical ethics corresponds to a moral psychology as advocated by Kohlberg, this is not true with visional ethics. Rather, "...a psychology of character will need to be developed in which the roots of a coherence of vision, thought, feeling, and action can be discovered and the dynamics of change charted out."[44]

Dykstra develops his own ideas initially in relation to imagination. He contends that moral growth is not developmental in itself, but rather that the findings of the developmental theorists, such as Piaget and Kohlberg, point to certain human capacities which then may or may not be actualized in moral growth. The absence of capacities can hinder moral progress, but the mere presence of the capacity is no guarantee of moral maturity. "However, it takes place when our capacities are brought to bear in particular experiences and patterns of experience."[45]

Dykstra, then, speaks of moral growth as intimately connected with human imagination. For him, imagination is the foundation stone for perception, understanding, and interpretation and, thus, for our understanding of the mystery of life, of all reality, and of God which confronts us. Imagination is very important in the process of coming to moral maturity. This relationship, of course, will not work itself out in ways that are contrary to reason and do not make sense. Rather, images enable us to see more deeply into the true nature of all reality. Dykstra contends that there is a certain dynamic to imaginal transformation. He sees a two-part process: a first movement which he calls discovery, and the later which he refers to as verification. While juridicial ethics seems to put the stress on verification, Dykstra would see an important role for intuition in discovering the nature of reality.

For Dkystra, then, moral growth involves a transformation of the imagination. This is not to preclude other important elements in coming to moral maturity, but it is to say that the transformation of the imagination is a rather important element in moral growth.

A very striking part of Dykstra's work centers around the three disciplines which he sees as very significant for the growth of Christian character. These disciplines are repentance, prayer and service. They seem to him "fundamental and generic" to moral progress. For him, repentance is not just a reorientation, but rather a complete transformation of the self. This transformation, of course, relates intrinsically to the prayer life of the person. "We need to pray for our repentance, and repentance makes possible better prayer. The two build on and nourish each other. But there is a sense in which prayer follows upon repentance."[46] The final discipline is service, which, of course, is related to the other two. Service involves a certain presence to others. In it 'we renounce power in order to be with others in vulnerability, in equality, and especially in compassion.

Through these three disciplines, we begin to deepen or to progress, or, more specifically, to be transformed in moral imagination. We grow morally when our capacities are transformed in and through these three disciplines. Repentance, prayer and service can take place at any stage of moral growth. However, as our capacities mature and we confront the complexities of life, we can grow in repentance, prayer and service. There is, however, no guarantee that this will happen. In fact, Dykstra explicitly mentions that it is possible not to develop at any stage—to lapse into a moral egoism or self-centeredness. It is also possible, morally speaking, to regress, to retreat, to go backward rather than forward in our moral state, in our moral character. As a person passes through the natural stages of growth, then, he or she can come to a more profound and deeper maturity, or lapse into moral weakness, or self-centeredness.

Dykstra sees all of the foregoing as having great implications for Christian education. He sees here an important role for the community in forming Christian character.

A community shapes our perceptions, values, and identities by the many subtle ways it uses language, sets norms, makes decisions and carries out actions. All that I am adding to their insights here is a criterion by which the adequacy of a community's socialization processes may be judged. That criterion is the depth of its engagement in the disciplines of the moral life.[47]

As the Christian educator seeks to help others to develop Christian character, Christian attitudes and Christian actions, he or she needs to respect the mystery of the individual. Education is not merely a matter of applying certain techniques to a situation. Rather, it is a process which respects the deep mystery and integrity of the individual. This process deeply involves the community, of course, but is not negligent when it comes to universalizable aspects of human experience. These need to be taken into consideration, but the focus is on the moral integrity or character of the person. Action manifests the quality of a person's moral life and flows from the progress one has made in moral development. This development, of course, involves the interpretation of one's surroundings and interaction with them. Thus, action flows from the character of the person, a dynamic character which, hopefully, continues to develop. Moral progress can continue throughout the cycle of human life and involves, of course, the discipline of repentance, prayer and service in a special way.

Dykstra's work, as can easily be seen, represents a reflection on and elaboration of the ground-breaking work of Hauerwas and others. It fleshes out in particularly Christian ways the contemporary analysis of moral character. Dykstra offers a profound and necessary reflection on imagination and vision as they relate to the moral life.

Dykstra's work, however, might be faulted in its stringent criticism of Kohlberg.[48] The data provided by Kohlberg needs to be more rigorously accounted for than Dykstra does in his presentation. Likewise, the criticisms made of Hauerwas in relation to the importance of individual acts need to be noted again here. The relationship of the individual act to the character of the person needs to be further delineated and expressed in concrete terms. These criticisms do not vitiate or weaken substantially the contribution that Dykstra has made, but rather point to areas for further reflection and integration.

Conclusion

As we can see from the preceding pages, reflection on Christian virtue is coming to have a significant place in contemporary Protestant ethics. The exact outcome of this renewed interest is not clear at the present time. However, there is room here for a substantial growth over the coming years. The vigor of theologians such as Moltmann, Hauerwas and Dykstra points to possibilities for a continued development. There are, of course, a number of areas that need to be further explored and significant alternatives need to be laid out. The convergence of interest in both Protestant and Catholic circles is quite striking and leads one to speculate that the ethics of character/virtue might be an area of significant ecumenical development for Christian ethics.

Having discussed the thought of numerous contemporary Catholic and Protestant theologians on Christian character or virtue, it now is appropriate to turn to the insights of certain developmental psychologists. These psychologists offer some interesting reflections on the growth of virtue. These reflections of contemporary psychology are already beginning to be incorporated into Christian reflection on virtue, the spiritual life, and moral growth and development. It is appropriate, then, to turn to the work of Erik Erikson, Lawrence Kohlberg and others in order to begin to grasp the essential elements of their theorizing which impact on, or perhaps could impact on, the ongoing work in the ethics of Christian character.

3
Developmental
Approaches—
Virtue and the Life Cycle

The approaches to virtue in the previous two chapters indicate the breadth of virtue-thinking and its contemporary ecumenical thrust. Reflection about the virtues of Christian living offers exciting possibilities for future ecumenical cooperation and investigation. Such thinking at the present time, however, seems to be in its infancy. Much work remains to be initiated and followed through to completion. The focus of virtue theory needs to include also the best in present-day studies.

One powerful current in contemporary thinking concerns itself with human growth and development. Investigation of the life cycle of the human person has attracted notable scientific interest. The popular mind in America has been greatly influenced by concern for "passages" and "pathways" through the decisive incidents and encounters of human living. This scientific and popular interest has its resonance in the circles of Christian theologians and religious educators. There is an increasing interest in integrating the solid findings of developmental psychologists into Christian theology and education. The burden of this and the following chapter will be to look at some virtue theories which show the influence of developmental thinking. The present chapter will investigate the psychosocial theory of Erik Erikson and its impact on virtue theory. The subsequent chapter will examine Lawrence Kohlberg's well-known work on stages of development of justice and James Fowler's recent work on the stages of faith.

The Use of Social Sciences in Moral Theology

Before considering the impact of developmental psychology on recent Christian virtue-thinking, it is important to examine briefly the use of the social sciences in theology. Recent years have seen significant efforts by both Catholic and Protestant authors to integrate the data of contemporary psychology into theology. This has been especially true in the areas of spiritual theology and Christian ethics, where theologians continue to investigate the psychological presuppositions for and concomitants of spiritual and moral growth as well as the obstacles to personal insight and responsibility. To achieve a thorough and valid integration, however, some ongoing reflection is neccessary on the nature of the data being considered and the process of assimilation. Such integration is not easy and has its pitfalls. Thus, caution and good judgment are called for in attempting to make the necessary integration.

In the last two decades, philosophers of science and scientists themselves have become aware of the role that presuppositions play in the development of scientific theories even in the "hard" sciences. Thomas Kuhn, in his book *The Structure of Scientific Revolutions,* presented a penetrating, if somewhat flawed, analysis of the life and death of the scientific paradigms which guide scientists in their work.[1] More recently, Allan Buss has seen himself as being in line with Kuhn's ideas as he discusses what he calls the sociology of psychological knowledge. He argues that psychology is practiced in a social context and that, by examining this context and its influences, psychologists will come to a greater self-understanding.[2] Furthermore, Norma Haan contends that psychological investigation of morality cannot separate description and evaluation and so cannot be value neutral. Thus she seeks for a reasonable way to deal with this inherently subjective element.[3]

All this is not to say that the traditional canons of science are unimportant. Rather, there is an objectivity to science, and even social sciences have not "... been proved irremediably subjective in both their means and their ends."[4] There are both objective and subjective factors intertwined in both the "hard" and "soft" sciences. The social sciences such as psychology, however, would seem to be more open to subjective factors. The important point here is that the individual and social values of the psychologists under consideration have to be allowed for. This does not invalidate their data and their theorizing, but merely makes one more circumspect in using such data.

Similar circumspection is called for in integrating psychology and spiritual or moral theology. As Robert Doran has mentioned in regard to spirituality, two extremes need to be avoided. One is the reduction of spirituality to psychology and the second is the divorce of psychology and spirituality. Doran argues that the two worlds are joined in the realm of interior experience.[5] The two are closely related and cannot easily be separated.

Psychology and theology can and should be integrated. But, in making this integration, several further cautions in addition to those just mentioned have to be put forward. First, as James Gustafson says,

In many instances the empirical studies used in moral theology and social ethics were not designed to help the moralist answer his questions; the stud-

ies were not done to resolve the moral questions.
Thus, the studies are in a profound sense "translated" from their own area of purpose to another.[6]

In using empirical studies, one must be sensitive to such a
change in context which may nuance considerably the con-
clusions that can be drawn from the data. Second, there are
many schools of psychological thought, and thus one needs
to be aware in some fashion of divergent viewpoints within
the field of psychology itself. Third, as Charles E. Curran
puts it, "The limitation of any individual science...arises
from the fact that an individual science by its very nature
does not encompass all aspects of the human reality."[7] That
is, psychological science, while profound, is limited in its
scope, and thus certain aspects of theology may have no
counterparts in psychology.

Finally, it must be noted that psychology is a *descriptive* science, concerned with the causes of human behavior.
Christian theology, on the other hand, is a *normative* discipline, concerned with the way in which human persons
summoned to life eternal with God ought to act in response
to the divine call to holiness. Spiritual writers like St. Francis de Sales and St. Teresa of Avila, for example, take for
granted the transcendent value of the human person and the
normative teaching of the Christian community.[8]

After presenting these few cautionary notes, one might
now say a few words on procedure. Paul Philibert argues
persuasively that:

When theology *borrows* from the social sciences,
the theologian must perform the act of seeing the
scientific conclusion within its own methodological
framework, judge the matter within its own frame of
reference, and only then appropriate it as a datum

within theology's framework—which will include, of course, placing it alongside other data not available to the empiricist, as well as receiving it on the terms of the very different methodology of theology.[9]

The theologian here would try to understand the data of psychology within its own frame of reference and evaluate it within that frame. This process would include, where applicable, reference to critical studies by other social scientists which contest or nuance the data under consideration. Then, having judiciously weighed the information presented by psychologists, the theologian would seek to situate it within and show its relation to a theological framework.

Theology and psychology can each shed light on the other. That is, theology brings its own positive contribution to the dialogue with psychology. It is not merely a matter of psychological insights modifying theological positions, but rather a matter of reciprocal interaction. The descriptive data and explanatory concepts of psychology, for example, might enable the theologian to grasp more readily the nature of human reality, while belief in a good and creative God might add a deeper sensitivity and reverence to the empirical study of the human developmental processes which are his handiwork.

One can see a general example of this interaction when Curran argues that the Christian view (1) of the future (eschatology) and (2) of human sinfulness limits the extent to which the data presented by empirical science can furnish norms of acting.[10] More particularly, Philibert, in discussing the relation of the work of Jean Piaget, Lawrence Kohlberg and other developmental psychologists to morality and moral education, contends that "...certain doctrines of Christian faith can offer to the believer insight and direction about the maturation of adult morality."[11]

The approach advocated here is one of mutual interaction and reciprocal modification.[12] This is not to say that there may not be some substantial differences between theology and modern psychology, but only to say that one can and should attempt to point out the light these disciplines shed on one another.

Thus, as we proceed to examine the efforts of contemporary psychologists and theologians in the subsequent sections, we will attempt to note in a critical and reflective manner how the two fields can be fruitfully integrated.

Erikson's Psychosocial Theory

One of the leading developmental psychologists in the United States is Erik Erikson. His work on the life cycle is a standard point of reference for developmental studies, especially those concerned with adolescents and adults. His eight psychosocial stages, spanning infancy to old age, offer a useful framework for conceiving the process of human growth.

In his thinking, Erikson maintains close ties to the psychoanalytic system in which he was trained even while he passes beyond it and adds to it. In particular, he retains many traditional psychoanalytic concepts such as the unconscious, regression, transference, libidinal disbalance, etc. in his clinical work. He finds such concepts quite useful in what he is doing. Among the concepts on which he puts a particular stress is the role of the *unconscious.* For him, "...every human expression means more than it seems to say...."[13] Such meaning can be of crucial significance for a person. That is, while seemingly determined by one conscious emotion, a person's relationships and acts are often unconsciously co-determined by their opposites. Acts mean more than they seem to say.

Building on psychoanalytic conceptualizations, Erikson has gradually come to enunciate his own theory. He uses clinical observations and insights to build his system, and he is wary of any excessive concern with objectivity. The ethical sentiments of the therapist, for example, are valuable both for clinical practice and in theory construction. Such relativity or subjectivity is not alien to science, but rather is necessary in coming to truly helpful knowledge. Erikson likes to speak of insight:

> This is a form of discernment hard to define and harder to defend, for it includes those preconscious assumptions which both precede and follow proven knowledge and formulated theory, and it includes enlightened common sense and informed partisanship. Without all of these, the clinician can neither heal nor teach; while he often comes face to face with his insights only in the act of interpreting, advising, or, indeed, lecturing. By then, however, he may find himself formulating conceptions which must again be verified in systematic observation.[14]

In advocating both subjective and objective knowledge from insight, Erikson has pulled away from his psychoanalytic moorings and gradually come to develop his own system.

In his approach, Erikson is concerned with the process of human life as it manifests itself in particular aspects. These might be classified very generically as the somatic process, the societal process, and the ego process.

> On the basis of case-historical and life-historical experience, therefore, I can only begin with the assumption that a human being's existence depends at every moment on three processes of organization that must complement each other. There is, in whatever order, the biological process of the hierarchic organi-

zation of organ systems constituting a body *(soma)*; there is the psychic process organizing individual experience by ego-synthesis *(psyche)*; and there is the communal process of the cultural organization of the interdependence of persons *(ethos)*.[15]

For Erikson these three processes relate together, and to understand any one human event completely an understanding of all three must be attained. These processes should not be seen in isolation, and any attempt to understand them individually will be inherently limited.

In speaking of the somatic process, Erikson speaks of what is inherent in the organism. Here in particular he mentions *epigenesis*. This principle of epigenesis is central to an understanding of Erikson's stages of development.

When we try to understand growth, it is well to remember the *epigenetic principle* which is derived from the growth of organisms *in utero*. Somewhat generalized, this principle states that anything that grows has a *ground plan* and that out of this ground plan, the *parts* arise, each part having its *time* of special ascendancy, until all parts have arisen to form a *functioning whole*.[16]

For Erikson the intervals of development create in the individual the potential for significant interaction for those around him or her. Some signficant potentialities only come to the fore later in life and thus beginnings, while very important, are not completely determinative.

In speaking of the societal process, Erikson is not speaking mainly of the family, but rather of the wider society. He believes that the community deeply affects the development of the individual and vice versa. Thus, his theory is known as psychosocial, for it is intended to complement and extend the psychosexual theory of Sigmund Freud. In thus making a strong place for the influence of society, Erikson is counteracting what he regards as the "originological fallacy." He believes that each child is potentially a new person and should not be thought to be determined by previous life influences unless there is a clear reason for doing so. This strong emphasis on the societal process, and thus on history, also leaves room for what Erikson calls "giftedness and grace." That is, some elements of human experience are beyond the explanation of psychological theorizing.

The third process in Erikson's thinking is the ego process. Generally, Erikson is considered to be an ego psychologist because of his emphasis on this process. Erikson sees the ego in terms which go beyond the original definition of Freud. The ego for him is the organizing principle in the person's experience and action. It is indispensable to the individual and his or her individuality. The ego is the balancing function in mental life and keeps things in perspective and yet it is ready for action. The ego mediates between outer events and inner responses. It maintains the sense that we are central in the flux of our own experience.[17] The ego is an active agent of synthesis and thus integrates the disparate elements of our human experience. It is central to the formation and sustenance of human personality and human identity. In order to maintain the human vision of wholeness, however, the ego for Erikson engages in certain delusions which, if punctured, can lead to the release of destructive rage related to the person's instinctual life. Thus, Erikson accounts not only for integration but for the destructive consequences of human instincts being released.

Stages of Moral Growth

After exposing briefly some central elements of Erikson's thinking, we might proceed now to investigate the stages that he proposes. These stages are outlined on the accompanying chart.[18] It should be noted that in his most recent work *The Life Cycle Completed*, Erikson investigates the stages moving from the last to the first. Here, however, we will follow the normal procedure in discussing them from early childhood to old age.

It is well to note at the outset that one's progress through these stages is not necessarily conscious either for children or for adults. They penetrate both surface and depth, embracing conscious and unconscious factors. In the charting, the

> Squares of the diagonal [signify] both a sequence of stages and a gradual development of component parts: in other words, the chart formalizes a progression through time of a differentiation of parts. This indicates (1) that each critical item of psychosocial strength ... is systematically related to all others, and that they all depend on the proper development in the proper sequence of each item; and (2) that each item exists in some form before its critical time normally arrives.[19]

The items in the diagonal constitute what are normally called the crises of development. By crisis, Erikson means a critical point, a time of transition. The successful resolution of one crisis prepares one to deal with the next. Previous resolutions are integrated into ongoing development. Toward the end of each stage the crisis, if it is resolved at all, comes to some form of resolution. The given life period is the

Chart 1

STAGES	A PSYCHOSEXUAL STAGES AND MODES	B PSYCHOSOCIAL CRISES	C RADIUS OF SIGNIFICANT RELATIONS	D BASIC STRENGTHS	E CORE-PATHOLOGY BASIC ANTIPATHIES	F RELATED PRINCIPLES OF SOCIAL ORDER	G BINDING RITUALIZATIONS	H RITUALISMS
I Infancy	Oral-Respiratory, Sensory-Kinesthetic (Incorporative Modes)	Basic Trust vs. Basic Mistrust	Maternal Person	Hope	Withdrawal	Cosmic Order	Numinous	Idolism
II Early Childhood	Anal-Urethral, Muscular (Retentive-Eliminative)	Autonomy vs. Shame, Doubt	Parental Persons	Will	Compulsion	"Law and Order"	Judicious	Legalism
III Play Age	Infantile-Genital Locomotor (Intrusive, Inclusive)	Initiative vs. Guilt	Basic Family	Purpose	Inhibition	Ideal Prototypes	Dramatic	Moralism
IV School Age	"Latency"	Industry vs. Inferiority	"Neighborhood," School	Competence	Inertia	Technological Order	Formal (Technical)	Formalism
V Adolescence	Puberty	Identity vs. Identity Confusion	Peer Groups and Outgroups; Models of Leadership	Fidelity	Repudiation	Ideological Worldview	Ideological	Totalism
VI Young Adulthood	Genitality	Intimacy vs. Isolation	Partners in friendship, sex, competition, cooperation	Love	Exclusivity	Patterns of Cooperation and Competition	Affiliative	Elitism
VII Adulthood	(Procreativity)	Generativity vs. Stagnation	Divided Labor and shared household	Care	Rejectivity	Currents of Education and Tradition	Generational	Authoritism
VIII Old Age	(Generalization of Sensual Modes)	Integrity vs. Despair	"Mankind" "My Kind"	Wisdom	Disdain	Wisdom	Philosophical	Dogmatism

ideal time for resolving a particular crisis. Resolutions achieved at a later date are usually very arduous. In coming to resolve the crisis of a particular stage, a person comes to a balance of competing possibilities. What is desired is a positive resolution of the varied crises of life. However, a completely positive resolution is neither possible nor desirable. Erikson believes that some elements of negativity can be helpful as one goes through the life cycle. For example, there is need for an element of distrust in life to enable one not to be taken advantage of by others. Thus, negative and positive are combined, but with the accent on the positive.

The stages themselves are rooted in Freud's psychosexual stages. They also have psychosocial roots as noted above, and thus are deeply influenced by the community. The stages may be passed through with variations of tempo and intensity. An individual or a culture may pass through the stages at an accelerated or decelerated rate and such a changed pace presumably will have modifying influence on each subsequent stage. The stages, too, are not discrete but rather overlap. A person cannot easily be neatly located at a given stage. Usually people oscillate between stages, at least until they move definitively into a higher one, at which point the stage beyond that even then begins to become operative. It is always important here to keep in mind that Erikson stresses that what one desires is a favorable ratio of positive to negative in coming to a resolution of a crisis. There is a need for a balance of what he calls the syntonic and dystonic tendencies at each of the stages. It is in conjunction with the resolution of the crises that the virtues, or, as he now calls them, human strengths, of the person will emerge.

Finally, it is important to be aware that the resolution of a stage is not an achievement which is secured once and for all, but rather becomes a part of the person's ongoing development. Hence, there is a certain sense of uprootedness concomitant with progress through the life stages.

These general comments of an introductory nature lead naturally to some consideration of the individual stages themselves. These considerations do not encompass all that Erikson has said in regard to the individual stages. But they do give a sense of the significant development of each stage.

STAGE 1.   *Trust vs. Mistrust*

This first stage dominates infancy. Trust is established usually in relationship to a maternal person. The development of trust depends primarily on the quality of this relationship. The mother's sensitive care combined with a sense of personal trustworthiness creates a framework in which the child can become a trusting person. This trust is a basic fundament of religion. "Parenthood faith," says Erikson, "... has throughout history sought its institutional safeguard (and, on occasion, found its greatest enemy) in organized religion."[20] Trust in Erikson's view is deeply related to religion.

STAGE 2.   *Autonomy vs. Shame and Doubt*

As the child moves into early childhood, his or her muscular structure progresses and he or she becomes capable of anal control and of standing on his or her own feet. The child's parents' own dignity as individuals reflects in their treatment of the child at this stage, and thus in the child's sense of autonomy. The shame which the child is protected from is the sense of self-consciousness, a sense of being exposed and being looked at, while the doubt has especially to do with having a "behind," a dark place not under one's control. The institutional safeguard of this stage is the principle of law and order. The individual will is affirmed here by the adult law and order of things. The child at this stage develops a sense of self-control.

STAGE 3.   *Initiative vs. Guilt*

At this stage the child comes more to a sense of himself or herself that is full of energy. The child is quick to approach that which is desirable and forgets failures quickly. The child at this stage takes pleasure in aggression such as an attack or conquest. The child, too, will make things along with others and will learn things quickly. The negative side of this stage is a sense of guilt over things thought and acts performed in the exhiliration of new mobility, energy, and understanding. It is at this stage that the child begins the long process which leads to becoming a bearer of the tradition. The social institutions at this stage offer to the child certain ideal adults who can be recognized by their uniform and function. These offer children an economic ethos in which to develop.

STAGE 4.   *Industry vs. Inferiority*

At this juncture a child learns how to be busy learning something and how to work with others. Here the child enters into school life, either in the formal schooling of the classroom or the less formal schooling of the field, and learns to conform himself or herself to the impersonal world of things, even of the 3 R's. In all cultures, the child receives some systematic instruction. The danger at this stage is that the child will develop a sense of inferiority and inadequacy. If the child despairs of his or her ability to use instruments or to work with others, then the person may become discouraged and develop a sense of inferiority. This may lead to a regression to a prior stage of development. It is at this level that the child learns to get a sense of the technological ethos which pervades a culture, whether this is primitive or highly developed.

STAGE 5.   *Identity vs. Role Confusion*

This is an area where Erikson has made a major contribution. Yet, he does not give a precise definition of identity.

He likes to use the term with many connotations that hint at its meaning. So at times he speaks of it as a sense of individual identity, at others a continuity of personal character, at others in reference to ego synthesis, and, finally, in still others as a sense of inner solidarity with the group's ideals and identity.[21] Identity is not conformist in the sense of merely surrendering to available social roles. The healthy individual adapts these roles to his or her own ego processes.

The sense of identity provides a personal feeling of inner continuity and sameness within the individual. Ego identity is characterized by an attained but continually revised sense of self within the social order. Erikson emphasizes too the psychosocial roots of identity. Personal identity needs to be firmly rooted in cultural identity and vice versa. The synthesis of personal and social is accomplished by the ego. One who has achieved ego identity is flexible and is able to deal with change, even radical change, because a well established identity is based on essential transcultural values.

When a person cannot achieve a positive sense of identity, he or she experiences what Erikson calls "identity confusion." This is a serious problem. It often manifests itself in connection with achieving sexual identity, with making a choice of occupation, with experiencing energetic competition, or with achieving psychosocial self-definition. These areas often occur in combination. Reversal of the process of identity confusion is a difficult task. Dealing with the problem begins with the willingness to accept the inevitability of certain personal realities. Psychoanalysis can help the client to restore this productive interplay between historical actuality and psychological reality.

STAGE 6. *Intimacy vs. Isolation*
This stage is the first of the stages of adult development. The stage of true intimacy assumes a positive resolu-

tion of the crisis of identity. Once identity is achieved, only then is one free to lose it in intimacy. Intimacy involves "...the capacity to commit himself to concrete affiliations and partnerships and to develop the ethical strength to abide by such commitments, even though they may call for significant sacrifices and compromises."[22] Since this is the age of adult genitality, the relationships spoken of are usually heterosexual in nature. But this does not preclude other relationships of depth in a person's life.

The danger here is that of isolation or distanciation. The avoidance of such experiences as close affiliations, sexual unions, close friendships, physical combat, inspiration by a teacher, etc. can lead to isolation and a self-absorption which is contrary to intimacy.

The primacy of genital sexuality at this stage might lead one to assume that this alone assures adult maturity. This, however, is not the case. Genitality needs to be a part of erotic intimacy, which in turn is part of shared generative commitment which leads to maturity.

STAGE 7.   *Generativity vs. Stagnation*

Intimacy flows naturally and necessarily into generativity. Generativity here has a wide meaning which includes the popular meaning of productivity and creativity. Generativity involves concern for the next generation, whether directly or through altruistic concern and creativity. By instinct and custom, adults at the generative stage forget death so that they may nourish their own kind.

On the negative side, Erikson sees a certain stagnation which is quite deadly, and which can be more specified as rejectivity, a suppression of what seems to go against one's "kind." This destructiveness may express itself even against one's children or those of others or in wars and other types of annihilation.

There is no one institution which can be singled out as codifying the ethics of generative succession. All institutions in some way are involved in this stage.

STAGE 8. Ego Integrity vs. Despair

This final stage of human life is the least clearly defined of Erikson's stages and the one least supported in the psychological literature. It embraces the person's adaptation to the successes and failures of life and thus is the fruit of the previous seven stages. Like the other stages, it has its roots deep in the preconscious and unconscious. Despair and disgust, too, are merely the most recent manifestation of the fear, anxiety and dread evident in the previous life stages.

For Erikson an integrated person does not fear death, and this helps children not to fear life. Integrity also has a religious dimension. The end of the life cycle is a time when certain "ultimate concerns" become evident—concerns to transcend the limits of identity and of the life cycle. The religious person is a person who is older or seems to be older in a sense that he or she is more taken up with these ultimate concerns, such as "...the question of how to escape corruption in living and how in death to give meaning to life."[23] The religious person often has a clearer perception of this earlier in life than does the normal person.

Basic Strengths or Virtues

In light of this discussion of the eight stages, we move now to consider the virtues of the life cycle. Erikson contends that certain basic strengths develop through human mutuality. Without these strengths all other human values and goodnesses would lack vitality. These basic human qualities develop in the interplay of successive generations

and safeguard the psychosocial survival of humanity as
well as the vibrancy of morals and ethics. "I will call 'virtue,'
then, certain human qualities of strength, and I will relate
them to that process by which ego strength may be developed from stage to stage and imparted from generation to
generation."[24]
  Erikson speaks of one basic virtue in connection with
each stage of the life cycle.

> I will, therefore, speak of *Hope, Will, Purpose*, and
> *Competence* as the rudiments of virtue developed in
> childhood; of *Fidelity* as the adolescent virtue; and
> of *Love, Care*, and *Wisdom* as the central virtues of
> adulthood. In all their seeming discontinuity, these
> qualities depend on each other. Will cannot be
> trained until hope is secure, nor can love become
> reciprocal until fidelity has proven reliable. Also,
> each virtue and its place in the schedule of all
> virtues is vitally interrelated to other segments of
> human development, such as the stages of psycho-
> sexuality which are so thoroughly explored in the
> whole of psychoanalytic literature, the psychoso-
> cial crises, and the steps of cognitive maturation.[25]

Erikson proceeds to give a definition of each of these
strengths of the ego. Hope arises from the child's contact
with a trustworthy maternal person who meets his or her
needs.

> *Hope is the enduring belief in attainability of primal
> wishes, in spite of the dark urges and rages which
> mark the beginning of existence and leave a lasting
> residue of threatening estrangement.*[26]

Hope, then, is the basis in development for what later becomes faith, a faith which is nourished by parental faith. This faith is not exclusively dependent upon reason though it embraces certain verifiable data and leads to a coherent role image.

The second strength of the life cycle is will. This is the stage of the genetic origin of that free will which has been the object of so much discussion throughout the centuries. *"Will, therefore, is the unbroken determination to exercise free choice as well as self-restraint, in spite of the unavoidable experience of shame and doubt in infancy."*[27] Will provides the basis for accepting both love and necessity.

The third virtue for Erikson is purpose. This is *"...the courage to envisage and pursue valued goals uninhibited by the defeat of infantile fantasies, by guilt and by the foiling fear of punishment."*[28]

The following virtue, that of competence or workmanship, appears as the child is learning the foundational principles of a productive way of life. It is *"...the free exercise of dexterity and intelligence in the completion of tasks, unimpaired by infantile inferiority."*[29]

The virtue of adolescence is fidelity. Like identity, fidelity is not a static formation, but rather a blend of continuity and of change. *"Fidelity is the ability to sustain loyalties freely pledged in spite of inevitable contradictions and confusions of value systems."*[30] It is a cornerstone of our human identity and it is opposed in adolescence by a certain naive cynicism.

Love is the virtue connected with the stage of intimacy. It is present in some way or other at every stage, but in a particular way it stands out here. The prerequisite for such love is a positive sense of identity and of fidelity. Love is *"...the mutuality of mates and partners in a shared identity,* for the mutual verification through an experience of finding oneself, as one loses oneself, in another."[31]

Intimately related to the virtue of love of the previous stage is that of care, the concomitant to the stage of generativity. Generativity and care, even as they are rooted in instinctive patterns, are also products of ego synthesis. *"Care is the widening concern for what has been generated by love, necessity, or accident; it overcomes the ambivalence adhering to irreversible obligation."*[32] Care can extend to a person's works and ideas as well as to one's children.

The final virtue of the life cycle is wisdom. *"Wisdom ...is detached concern with life itself, in the face of death itself."*[33]

This extended exposition has pointed out the various virtues of the different stages of the life cycle and has defined each of them. It should be reiterated that these virtues are to be seen as an integral part of Erikson's overall view. That is, they are anchored in epigenesis, in the sequence of generations, and in the growth of the ego. They grow as part of the ensemble and are reintegrated at later stages. They are intertwined with psychosexual and psychosocial development, and with cognitive development as well, and the strands cannot very easily be separated.

Virtues have their negative side which can be characterized by the term "weakness," with its associated symptoms of disorder, dysfunction, disintegration, and anomie. Weakness here seems to parallel the negative outcome of the eight developmental crises. Moreover, the development of virtue is essentially related to the human community, though Erikson does not spell this out in great detail. Erikson believes that, in discussing these virtues, he is not talking about any moral purpose built into nature, but rather speaking of the adaptive strengths inherent in the evolution of the life cycle.

Reflections on Erikson's Theory

The foregoing exposition of Erikson's theory of psychosocial development leads us to critically examine its content. A number of recent studies are built upon the work of Erikson. Daniel Levinson and his associates see Erikson's work as important background for their own. Likewise, George Vaillant in his longitudinal study, *Adaptation to Life,* finds Erikson's theory to be helpful and essentially valid. So, too, James Fowler sees Erikson's work as providing a significant basis for his own.[34] These authors, however, also go beyond Erikson's basis in their work. Levinson elaborates his own stages of adult development, while Vaillant adds several new dimensions in his own longitudinal study. For instance, he disputes Erikson's contentions about the importance of early childhood traumas. Vaillant contends that it is the quality of early life relationships rather than isolated traumas which are most significant for development. Fowler, too, moves away from Erikson's system, seeing it as a general background to his theory, and embraces the work of Piaget, Kohlberg, Selman and others as the foundation for his theory of faith development. The work of Erikson then is for many the touchstone for further elaborations and developments.

As mentioned earlier, Erikson's work is sketchy in regard to old age. His most recent book, *The Life Cycle Completed,* elaborates somewhat more on this stage, which Erikson himself has now reached, but does not really delineate it all that clearly. The findings on late adulthood seem to be disparate and there is a need for further work on this period.

Erikson's conceptions are also quite general in nature. There is some question as to how necessarily sequential his stages might be, particularly at the higher levels. There is a need, too, to delineate the previous and subsequent development of the individual stages—for example, what are the early forms of intimacy in the first five stages of the life cycle and what can be considered to be the later forms of intimacy after early adulthood. The stages are somewhat general in their descriptiveness and are quite helpful in counseling and in reflections on adult development. But this very generalness also inhibits one in dealing with the specificities of the individual stages. Thus, the stages need to be complemented with other forms of knowledge about adult development. This is not to deny the importance of Erikson's theory but rather to see it in its proper context.

There is a need for those who seek to use Erikson's theory from a religious perspective to realize the psychoanalytic moorings of the parts of this theory. This does not preclude its use, but rather should make us aware that any attempt to use his theory will involve an integration of elements not specific to Erikson's work. Erikson's conceptions will be translated into a religious framework and this should be kept in mind using his results.

The Influence of Erikson on Virtue Theory

Erikson's wide-ranging synthesis, which has just been explored cursorily, has had some impact on Christian reflection on virtue. James Fowler's work on faith development shows Erikson's general influence. So, too, does the synthetic work of the authors described below.

1. Meissner's Psychology of Grace

William W. Meissner, S.J. reflects upon stages of growth, but he does so from a psychological point of view. His concern is with the life of grace and the concomitant life of virtue as they affect man's psyche. His is not a theological but a psychological inquiry.

> If one can accept the proposition that grace is more than theologically operational, that it does have a psychological impact, then it should be possible to formulate that psychological impact. Grace does not merely change man's theological condition, changing him in reference to the supernatural, but it reaches into his very nature and makes contact with the deepest reaches of his psychic reality.[35]

Virtues, of course, are directly related to grace.

Meissner theorizes that the impact of grace is on the ego. Grace works "...in and through the resources of the ego."[36] It mobilizes or intensifies ego-strengths by making available independent ego-energies. In so doing, it subjects itself to the natural laws of development and operation of the ego.

For a person to come to full maturity, his or her ego must integrate spiritual realities and values; that is, he or she must achieve a spiritual identity. Just as a person achieves a certain identity in coming to psychological maturity, so too he or she achieves a spiritual identity in coming to spiritual maturity. The process of integration here, however, is ongoing and continuous because the spiritual realm can always be penetrated more profoundly. The spiritual, of course, builds on and is intertwined with the natural. There is a kind of reciprocal relationship between the two identities.

Meissner, following Erikson's general conceptualizations,[37] presents eight psychospiritual crises which attend the process of spiritual identity formation. Meissner's stages are:

1) Faith, hope	5) Humility
2) Contrition	6) Love of neighbor
3) Penance, temperance	7) Service, zeal, self-sacrifice
4) Fortitude	8) Charity[38]

Meissner envisions these psychospiritual stages as being more flexible than Erikson's psychosocial stages of development in that they depend on a completely gratuitous factor, God's grace. A person may not begin to pass through these stages until later in life.

Meissner seeks to link each of his psychospiritual stages to one of Erikson's eight stages of growth. He sees Erikson's stage as the usual precondition for his own stage. Thus, for example, with regard to Erikson's first stage of basic trust, Meissner believes that both faith and hope can build on this basic aspect of the personality. If trust is lacking, the development of faith and hope is impeded. Yet, there is a reciprocal influence at work here because grace is gratuitous.

> If the ego is able to commit itself in some degree through the energizing capacity of grace through faith and/or hope, the implied disposition of trust in God and confidence in Him will exercise a reciprocal influence on the orientation to basic trust in the personality. The extent to which this sanating influence will be realized depends on the intensity of the energizing effect of grace and on the degree to which the ego mobilizes its resources in responding to grace.[39]

Meissner makes similar remarks in seeking to connect each one of his stages to one of Erikson's.

Meissner sees his work as an initial attempt to formulate a psychology of grace. He believes that much remains to be done. This includes the development of a meaningful psychological understanding of Christian virtue, perhaps from an Eriksonian perspective.

2. The Attitude-Virtues of Donald Evans

A recent book (1979) by Donald Evans also shows the influence of Erikson's paradigm on the present-day discussion. Having initially been influenced by Erikson, Evans proceeds to build his own system of eight attitude-virtues. These arise from reflective common sense, psychoanalysis, and Christian spiritual teaching with the primary emphasis resting on the first two sources. The eight attitude-virtues in order are: trust, humility, self-acceptance, responsibility, self-commitment, friendliness, concern, and contemplation.[40] Evans proposes that these eight attitude-virtues are the prime constituents of religion and morality.

> In making such a proposal I am presupposing that religion is primarily a set of attitudes and that morality is primarily a set of virtues. I am also claiming that the eight attitude-virtues are the main constituents of human fulfillment.[41]

These attitude-virtues are sequential in nature, as are Erikson's stages. Each represents a pervasive stance which influences all behavior to a certain extent. These virtues have corresponding vices which exist in every person and cannot be completely eliminated. These "...can, however, be reduced by refusing to let it have full control in one's life and by being open to whatever fosters the opposing attitude-virtues."[42] Human fulfillment occurs when the virtues predominate.

Evans spends a great deal of time discussing trust, the basic attitude-virtue which has a profound impact throughout life. If a person is trustful, he or she can respond positively and creatively to self, others, and world. Trust pervades all one's encounters with others. Distrust, on the other hand, focuses on and perceives evil as characterizing the environment. It is preoccupied with the forces which undermine life rather than with those who promote it. Basic trust is the fundament of religious beliefs and of moral life in relationship with others. Trust unifies all of life, and all the other attitude-virtues depend on it.

Growth in each of its stages involves affirming the positive forces in one's life and resisting the forces of destruction. Few come to complete human fulfillment, but everyone can make progress. What is most significant is the direction in which one is going. The last three attitude-virtues, friendliness, concern and contemplation, in particular, are goals of the process.

> The eight attitude-virtues are connected in various ways. Friendliness and concern are each species of love and together they create a context for contemplation, which is also a species of love. The combination of all three is the supreme goal in human life, though the emphasis in the combination differs from person to person. The other five attitude-virtues are prerequisites for these three. Only insofar as we have a firm grasp on ourselves can we let go of ourselves in love.[43]

This emphasis on the centrality of love drawn from Evans' own experience and psychoanalysis converges with the traditional Christian perspective. Evans believes that his work is generally compatible with the tradition, but he does not attempt to prove this. He believes that the four cardinal virtues and many others besides are included either explicitly or implicitly in his system. He rejects, however, the distinction between theological and moral virtues.[44] His attitude-virtues, he contends, focus on both God and people.

Finally, one should note that Evans does not hold rigidly to the sequential nature of his virtues. He believes that often people skip around among stages. In particular "...my account of the three species of love is at best a *reminder* that all three are important and a *context* in which each individual can make his own decision concerning practical priorities among them."[45]

Evans' work is a quite provocative extension of Eriksonian ideas on virtue. His focus on the roots of the virtuous life in human experience is helpful, while the close linkage of attitudes and virtues seems open to question and certainly in need of further support. Hauerwas and Bondi, in reviewing Evans' work, appreciatively note that "...attitudes, virtues, and their reflective articulation are a good deal more complicated than Evans has assumed thus far."[46] His work, then, is capable of further refinement and could be related more explicitly to contemporary Christian thinking on virtue.

3. Christian Life Patterns—The Whiteheads' Contribution

Evelyn E. Whitehead and James D. Whitehead in their book *Christian Life Patterns* give an extended treatment to the Christian life as related to adult developmental psychology. Many of their concerns relate to the concerns of this chapter, though their thrust is much more toward understanding development and living the Christian life. They, too, are greatly influenced by Erikson, as were Meissner and

Evans; but they concentrate on the three crises of adult development, not only as presented by Erikson, but also as elaborated by Levinson, Vaillant, *et al.* They chart religious growth "... in terms of an adult's maturing sense of identity (discipleship), the ability to love and give of oneself (charity), and the capacity for responsible care (stewardship)."[47]

The Whiteheads see that spiritual growth involves change. They believe that God's grace is manifestly at work within the structures of adult growth. Some recent psychological studies have given more data on the general patterns of adult growth, and it is these which can be and are affected by God's grace. Grace can compress or extend the normal patterns of adult growth just as sin can retard or shatter such patterns. Growth, both spiritual and psychological, is, of course, not just a matter of response to the positive events of life, but also a matter of dealing with loss and failure in a constructive manner. Erikson points to certain psychological "virtues" as the strengths of the ego which attend the positive resolution of these life crises. The Whiteheads ask:

> How are these psychological virtues related to Christian virtue? In the Judaeo-Christian tradition virtue in its most basic sense refers to a faithfulness to God (Leon-Dufour, 1967). Whether expressed as obedience to the will of God or more lyrically as 'walking with God' (Gen. 5:22–24, 6:9), virtue describes the response of the believer to God's presence in life. For the contemporary Christian, we suggest, this presence can be discerned within the structure and tasks of adult growth—not only in its patterned unfolding but its crises and apparent disruptions of growth.[48]

Erikson's developmental scheme, in particular, can point to ways in which central Christian virtues such as charity and service present themselves in the Christian life. The committed Christian sees God's hand in the natural crises of growth and maturity.

> The belief that such a critical experience signals the inbreaking of God in my life, or that the decision to be made in an adult crisis has to do with God's plan for my future, is not an element in a psychological theory of development. Such an interpretation derives from the Christian vision; it is this vision that renders human development religious.[49]

The Whiteheads, then, offer some extended reflections on the relationship of adult developmental psychology to the Christian life. Theirs is a very worthwhile initial attempt at synthesis. As such it lacks the critical depth which usually emerges over time. The book tends to generalities, avoids extended critical analysis of the Eriksonian approach, and tends to present an integration with Christian spirituality *in globo*. Hence, there is a need to complement it with some specific studies that would relate developmental findings to the specific schools of Christian spirituality.

The writings of Meissner, Evans, and the Whiteheads show the significant impact which the theory of Erikson has had on Christian reflection on virtue. It is interesting to note the initial state of so much of this work. There is room for a great deal of further investigation into the relation of psychodynamics and life crises to progress in virtue. This continues to be a rich field open to further inquiries.

4
Structural-
Developmental
Approaches

The exposition in the previous chapter shows the importance of the psychosocial theory of Erik Erikson for some contemporary theories of virtue. The present chapter will investigate two structural developmental approaches to virtue. These are Lawrence Kohlberg's theory of moral development and James Fowler's work on faith development. Both of these virtue theories are structuralist in nature. They both rely on the groundbreaking work of Jean Piaget in offering their developmental theories of justice and faith. In so doing, they do not remain content with the work of Piaget, but rather go much beyond and in many ways modify and develop his theory. In all of this, they differ significantly from the psychosocial theories previously studied. Thus, the structural developmentalists make a suggestive and provocative contribution to contemporary reflection on virtue.

Kohlberg's Theory of Moral Development

The well-known theory of moral development of Lawrence Kohlberg presents a distinctive contribution to present-day discussion. Kohlberg proposes a six stage theory of moral development. This stage theory rests on his philosophical studies, his intuition, and his empirical investigations. Kohlberg began his work in 1958 with his doctoral dissertation. He continues to pursue this work up to the present day. He periodically revises his theory to fit the results of his ongoing investigations. The six stages, as recently described in his book on the philosophy of moral development, are as follows:

Level A: Preconventional Level

Stage One.   The Stage of Punishment and Obedience.
Right is literal obedience to rules and authority, avoiding punishment, and not doing physical harm. This stage takes an egocentric point of view.

Stage Two.   The Stage of Individual Instrumental Purpose and Exchange.
Right is serving one's own or others' needs and making fair deals in terms of concrete exchange. This stage takes a concrete individualistic perspective.

Level B: Conventional Level

Stage Three.   The Stage of Mutual Interpersonal Expectations, Relationships, and Conformity.
Right is playing a good (nice) role, being concerned about other people and their feelings, keeping loyalty and trust with partners, and being motivated to follow rules and expectations. This stage takes the perspective of the individual in relationship to other individuals.

Stage Four. The Stage of Social System and Conscience Maintenance.

Right is doing one's duty in society, upholding the social order, and maintaining the welfare of society or the group. This stage differentiates societal point of view from interpersonal agreement or motives.

Level C: Postconventional and Principled Level

Stage Five. The Stage of Prior Rights and Social Contract or Utility.

Right is upholding the basic rights, values, and legal contracts of a society, even when they conflict with the concrete rules and laws of the group. This stage takes a prior-to-society perspective—that of a rational individual aware of values and rights prior to social attachments and contracts.

Stage Six. The Stage of Universal, Ethical Principles.

This stage assumes guidance by universal, ethical principles that all humanity should follow. This stage takes the perspective of a moral point of view from which social arrangements derive, or on which they are grounded. The perspective is that of any rational individual recognizing the nature of morality or the basic premise of respect for other persons as ends, not means.[1]

Kohlberg comes to his stages through interviewing subjects and analyzing their responses to moral dilemmas. The person is presented with a story which describes a moral situation. He or she is asked to respond to the situation and then is probed for the reasoning behind the response. Through this method, Kohlberg has come to the six stages just presented. These stages show the structure of moral reasoning, not the content of particular decisions. Kohlberg wants to abstract from specific content. He believes that his stages are universal and that as a person develops he or she passes through these stages sequentially. Once one reaches a particular stage, the person will never regress.

Kohlberg also contends that basic moral principles are not directly related to religious beliefs. He and his associates have found no significant differences in moral development between believers of Christian and non-Christian persuasion and atheists.

Kohlberg's theory assumes that, at its root, moral development is structural. He also assumes that our growth comes from interaction. Interaction with the environment, and especially with others, forces the individual to restructure his or her experience and thus, hopefully, to advance. Kohlberg believes that:

Both psychological and philosophical analogies suggest that the more mature stage of moral thought is the more structurally adequate. This greater adequacy of more mature moral judgment rests on structural criteria more general than those of truth-value or efficiency. These general criteria are the *formal* criteria developmental theory holds as defining all mature structures, the criteria of increased differentiation and integration.[2]

Kohlberg singles out justice, a universal prescriptive principle, as the key virtue for moral growth. He supports the use of this principle by a philosophical analysis. He sees his work as related to the philosophy of Kant and to the recent philosophical efforts of John Rawls. Kohlberg points out that "...no principle other than justice has been shown to meet the formal conception of a universal, prescriptive principle."[3]

Justice ultimately, at stage six, even takes priority over other principles which concern human welfare. For him, justice is basically equality and reciprocity. It fits in this way: "(a) Moral judgment is a role-taking process which (b) has a logical structure at each stage, paralleling Piaget's logical stages; this structure is best formulated as (c) a justice structure, which (d) is progressively more comprehensive, differentiated, and equilibrated than the prior structure."[4] The development of the structure of justice depends also upon social interaction and cooperation. Thus, moral development is seen to involve both role taking and social interaction.

Justice appears here as the central virtue of individual moral development. Justice is not a virtue term which awards praise or blame to others. (Kohlberg scorns virtues such as these by referring to the "bag of virtues approach.") Justice develops in the interaction of the person with his or her surroundings. Justice here is considered more in a philosophical line, but has obvious relation to theological considerations. Kohlberg's work provides an interesting challenge to theology. Paul Philibert argues that the data collected by Kohlberg can be related to the Aristotelian-Thomistic tradition of virtue thinking.[5] He believes that this tradition can explain Kohlberg's data more comprehensively and that Kohlberg misunderstands the classical virtue-tradition in speaking of the "bag of virtues." Philibert, however, does not pursue this effort at recasting the Kohlberg system in classical Aristotelian-Thomistic terms.

Critical Evaluation of Kohlberg's Approach

The foregoing considerations of Kohlberg's basic theory of justice lead us now to some critical reflections. Kohlberg's theory is very interesting and it became very popular in the 1960s and 1970s, especially with religious educators, because it provided a different type of approach to morality and it could be practically applied. The approach now has been subject to a great deal of criticism, and it is important to be aware of that criticism and some other observations about Kohlberg's theory. Basically, the theory is very stimulating and interesting and has a fair amount of validity. There are a number of recent studies which back up Kohlberg's theory.[6] However, these studies tend to focus on younger people, children and adolescents. There is also a great deal of questioning of Kohlberg's system by psychologists and philosophers, religious educators and theologians.

One might look, first of all, at some of the psychological or methodological issues. Kohlberg has been criticized in a number of areas. First, he proposes a sequence of stages. It is disputed whether these are an invariant sequence, as he claims. At one point Kohlberg spoke about a stage 4½— halfway between 4 and 5—because there were young people, in late adolescence or early adulthood, who seemed to be retrogressing to stage 2. So he hypothesized a stage 4½ as a transition between stages 4 and 5. This whole question eventually led to further reflection on the meaning of stage 5 and the transition between stages. Some questions as to whether these stages are in fact universal have also arisen. The studies Kohlberg has done in Turkey and Mexico have been questioned because the paucity of information provided does not enable his fellow psychologists to replicate his work easily.

Another problem, which Kohlberg notes himself, is that

from 1968 to 1976 there has been no data that would back up the existence of stage 6.[7] This is a significant admission: there is no proof for stage 6. Stage 6 thus relies much more on philosophical considerations than on any type of empirical data, and, of course, this greatly weakens his argument for a universal moral principal orientation. Furthermore, if one goes a little further, questions can be raised about stage 5. There seems to be some information to back up stage 5, but Kohlberg himself, in speaking of moral education, is even going back to working on stage 4 in his Just Community School in Cambridge. (This is a high school which operates as a community to stimulate moral development.)

Another important issue is the whole question of relativism in content. Kohlberg argues that, while the structures are invariant, the contents of each stage can vary. However, one recent author argues that "...a neglect of other forms of moral cognition, especially the content of particular moral beliefs, is responsible for the theoretical obscurity and empirical confustion noted...in this area."[8] So there is some confusion and continual question about how content and structure relate together and whether it is possible, especially at the higher levels, to separate them. Here the whole relativism issue arises—how can a moral person come down on either side of a given issue? Can one so easily separate out, especially for the adult, structure from content?

These are some remarks that relate to the empirical basis of Kohlberg's theory. In this connection, it is appropriate to say a few words about the philosophical side of his work. Kohlberg adopts a certain school of thought, the deontology of Kant, as a philosophical foundation of his theory. Philosophers from other schools of thought would certainly question this choice. Both philosophers and psychologists argue that Kohlberg confuses the psychological and philosophical, that the dividing lines are not very clear in his system.[9] It also seems that the philosophical stance is not an outgrowth of the data, but rather that it entered in from the beginning. Thus, his is not purely an empirical theory and is subject to some questioning. Kohlberg, of course, is aware of these criticisms, and he argues, on the contrary, that you cannot separate the philosophical and psychological bases of his work. The two go together. They cannot be separated out as easily as people would like.

Third, we might consider the application of Kohlberg's theory to religious education, and implicitly to formation in virtue. Kohlberg has some good emphases: taking persons where they are and helping persons to develop their own reasoning power about moral issues. However, there is more to religious education than reasoning. There is the whole affective dimension, which is not prominent in Kohlberg's theory. He does attempt to deal with it, but most commentators feel that he does not deal with it sufficiently or convincingly. Furthermore, we come to the whole behavioral aspect of religious education. Religious educators wonder whether just thinking differently leads to acting differently. Behavior and training for behavior should be part of religious education apart from moral discussion. Likewise, too, there is the whole imaginative dimension, the symbolic dimension, and the liturgical dimension. All of these are part of religious education. Basically, there seems to be a consensus among many people reflecting on the issues that Kohlberg's work is necessary but not sufficient. There is more to moral development than Kohlberg allows.[10]

Finally, in regard to theology we might note a number of things. For example, Ralph Potter believes that Kohlberg narrows the account of what morality is all about by his theory and his methods. Potter thinks that Kohlberg has oversimplified things. The nature and contents of moral deliberation are oversimplified in Kohlberg's system. He very much overemphasizes the role of logic, Potter feels, as an influence on conduct. This leads to an impoverished view of what moral character is all about. This logical, very rational approach is inadequate. It neglects other important dimensions in moral life, such as vocation, because it focuses in on the one area of justice, the logic of moral development.[11]

Craig Dykstra adds to such considerations when he speaks of moral imagination as not being provided for in Kohlberg's formalistic system. Dykstra argues that Kohlberg's system should be left aside and develops an ethics of character as noted in Chapter 2 above. Most authors contend, however, that Kohlberg's work needs to be modified and supplemented rather than rejected. Paul Philibert, for example, a strong advocate of virtue ethics, believes that much can be learned from Kohlberg's work. He contends that one also must consider the relational elements that are the complement of the formalistic structures about which Kohlberg speaks. Thus, he says that we have to have a broader view, including Christian elements such as conversion and guidance by the Holy Spirit.

Gabriel Moran in his recent book *Religious Education Development*[12] devotes some consideration to Kohlberg's theory. He would like to see some more investigation of the mutual interplay between religion and morality, a possibly beneficial relationship that Kohlberg does not investigate. The religious dimension of Kohlberg's theory is stage seven, a kind of mystical stage beyond six. Stage six is universalizing principles for humanity, and stage seven is a cosmic mystical focus that brings everything together. It encompasses more than universality and is actually a grounding of universality on those things that cannot be handled by universal principles. It is rather vague, and Kohlberg does not develop it much. This stage seven is a religious stage. Moran argues that this relation of religion and morality needs to be explored much more than Kohlberg has done. Moran criticizes Kohlberg too on the issue of imagery and language. Kohlberg does not explore the imagery and language for describing moral development. He has no room for a circular or spiral movement or anything similar, no room for imagination or investigation of language. Kohlberg's system, then, might be supplemented or further developed by considering these varied elements.

Conclusion

These extensive criticisms of Kohlberg's theory are important and valid, but they do not eliminate his substantial contribution. While one might doubt the validity of Kohlberg's higher stages, there seems to be substantial evidence for his earlier ones. Thus, there is data which points out a development of an understanding of justice in early childhood and in adolescence. Kohlberg offers an insightful and helpful delineation of the development of justice. His work certainly needs to be complemented with the work of others, but his contribution cannot be doubted. His work has also been an inspiration to others, as will be seen in the theory of faith development to be discussed subsequently.

Stages of Faith: The Synthesis of James Fowler

After these extended considerations of the theory of justice of Lawrence Kohlberg, some attention needs to be focused on the creative work of James Fowler. Fowler presents an integrated and imaginative view of faith development which is having a wide impact in religious education and in theology. Fowler builds his theory of faith development on the work of Erik Erikson and the structural developmental theorizing of Piaget and Kohlberg. Fowler offers a unique and provocative synthesis which has a wide and deep power of explanation. Yet his work still needs a great deal of further elaboration. Even in its initial form, however, it has proved itself both helpful in pastoral counseling and religious education and provocative in its theological profundity.

Fowler investigates the human side of faith development. For him, faith is so fundamental that no one can live for long without it. Faith is a human universal. That is, it applies to all people in all cultures. It is the same phenomenon for Christians as well as for Marxists. Faith, for Fowler, is interactive and social. It requires a communtiy which provides language, ritual, and nurture. Faith, then, is not necessarily religious, in either its content or its context. Faith gives meaning to the relationships and forces which make up a human life. Faith is relational. That is, there is always an other, another person, in a faith relationship. Likewise, there are always centers of value and power which form the context of the interpersonal dimension of faith. This relational mode involves, or can involve, a relationship to the other who is the ultimate center for all values and of all power—that is, God. Finally, faith is a type or a kind of imagination. It forms a way of seeing our lives in relationship to the whole, or to our ultimate environment. The imaginative element in faith encompasses those emotional and affective elements which are so inadequately considered in Kohlberg's theory. For Fowler, "Faith, then, is an active mode of knowing, of composing a felt sense or image of the conditions of our lives taken as a whole. It unifies our lives' force fields."[13]

As can easily be seen, Fowler's definition of faith is quite wide ranging. His contribution, however, to the contemporary discussion of the virtue of faith lies not in his definition, or, perhaps more accurately, his description of faith, but in his proposal for stages of faith development. These six stages are sequential and cover the whole life cycle. Fowler's stages are in some ways modeled on those of Piaget and Kohlberg, but he believes that these faith stages cannot be reduced to either or both of these initial components. Fowler believes, however, that the stages which he has discovered in his research are truly structural and meet the structural-developmental criteria for stages. He believes these stages to be in an invariant sequence. Each subsequent stage reintegrates and develops operations of the previous stage. The stages, rather than being lost then, spiral upward in progressing toward a greater individuality by stage four and then looping back with an increased focus on community in stages five and six. Fowler does not claim at this time that his stages are universal. Rather, he hopes that they are, but realizes that he has no empirical data to support this supposition.

Fowler's theory is based on interviews conducted by Fowler himself and his associates over the last ten years. It is from the interview material, which includes upward of four hundred interviews, that Fowler derives his six stages of faith development. Each of these stages can be characterized by seven aspects (See accompanying Table.) These aspects are: (1) the form of logic, based on Piaget's work, (2) the form of perspective, taken from the work of Robert Selman, (3) the form of moral judgment (Kohlberg), (4) the bounds of social awareness, (5) the locus of authority, (6) the form of world coherence, and finally (7) the symbolic function.[14] These aspects which relate to the description of faith mentioned above form the structure of the stages of faith.

Fowler in his most recent exposition describes the stages in these terms:

Chart 2. Faith Stages by Aspects

ASPECT:	A. Form of Logic (Piaget)	B. Perspective Taking (Selman)	C. Form of Moral Judgment (Kohlberg)	D. Bounds of Social Awareness	E. Locus of Authority	F. Form of World Coherence	G. Symbolic Function
STAGE:							
I	Preoperational	Rudimentary empathy (egocentric)	Punishment-reward	Family, primal others	Attachment/dependence relationships. Size, power, visible symbols of authority	Episodic	Magical Numinous
II	Concrete Operational	Simple perspective taking	Instrumental hedonism (Reciprocal fairness)	"Those like us" (in familial, ethnic, racial, class and religious terms)	Incumbents of authority roles, salience increased by personal relatedness	Narrative-Dramatic	One-dimensional; literal
III	Early Formal Operations	Mutual Interpersonal	Interpersonal expectations and concordance	Composite of groups in which one has interpersonal relationships	Consensus of valued groups and in personally worthy representatives of belief-value traditions	Tacit system, felt meanings symbolically mediated, globally held	Symbols multi-dimensional; evocative power inheres in symbol
IV	Formal Operations (Dichotomizing)	Mutual, with self-selected group or class —(Societal)	Societal perspective, Reflective relativism or class-biased univeralism	Ideologically compatible communities with congruence to self-chosen norms and insights	One's own judgment as informed by a self-ratified ideological perspective. Authorities and norms must be congruent with this.	Explicit system, conceptually mediated, clarity about boundaries and inner connections of system.	Symbols separated from symbolized. Translated (reduced) to ideations. Evocative power inheres in *meaning* conveyed by symbols.

V	Formal Operations (Dialectical)	Mutual with groups, classes and traditions "other" than one's own	Prior to society, Principled higher law (universal and critical)	Extends beyond class norms and interests. Disciplined ideological vulnerability to "truths" and "claims" of outgroups and other traditions	Dialectical joining of judgment-experience processes with reflective claims of others and of various expressions of cumulative human wisdom.	Multisystemic symbolic and conceptual mediation	Postcritical rejoining of irreducible symbolic power and ideational meaning. Evocative power inherent in the reality in and beyond symbol and in the power of unconscious processes in the self.
VI	Formal Operations (Synthetic)	Mutual, with the commonwealth of being	Loyalty to being	Identification with the species. Transnar-cissistic love of being	In a personal judgment informed by the experiences and truths of previous stages, purified of egoic striving, and linked by disciplined intuition to the principle of being.	Unitive actuality felt and participated unity of "One beyond the many"	Evocative power of symbols actualized through unification of reality mediated by symbols and the self.

In the pre-stage call undifferentiated faith, the seeds of trust, courage, hope and love are fused in an undifferentiated way and contend with sensed threats of abandonment, inconsistencies and deprivations in an infant's environment. Though really a pre-stage and largely inaccessible to empirical research of the kind we pursue, the quality of mutuality and the strength of trust, autonomy, hope and courage (or their opposites) developed in this phase underlie (or threaten to undermine) all that comes later in faith development.

Stage 1. Intuitive-Projective faith is the fantasy filled, imitative phase in which the child can be powerfully and permanently influenced by examples, moods, actions and stories of the visible faith of primally related adults.

The stage most typical of the child of three to seven, it is marked by a relative fluidity of thought patterns.

The gift or emergent strength of this stage is the birth of imagination, the ability to unify and grasp the experience-world in powerful images and as presented in stories that register the child's intuitive understandings and feelings toward the ultimate conditions of existence.

Stage 2. Mythic-Literal faith is the stage in which the person begins to take on for him- or herself the stories, beliefs and observances that symbolize belonging to his or her community. Beliefs are appropriated with literal interpretations, as are moral rules and attitudes. Symbols are taken as one-dimensional and literal in meaning. The episodic quality of Intuitive-Projective faith gives way to a more linear, narrative construction of coherence and meaning. This is the faith stage of the school child (though we sometimes find the structures dominant in adolescents and in adults). Marked by increased accuracy in taking the perspective of other persons, those in Stage 2 compose a world based on reciprocal fairness and an immanent justice based on reciprocity.

Stage 3. Synthetic-Conventional faith, a person's experience of the world, now extends beyond the family. Faith must provide a coherent orientation in the midst of that more complex and diverse range of involvements. Faith must synthesize values and information; it must provide a basis for identity and outlook.

Stage 3 typically has its rise and ascendancy in adolescence, but for many adults it becomes a permanent place of equilibrium. It structures the ultimate environment in interpersonal terms. Its images of unifying value and power derive from the extension of qualities experienced in personal relationships. It is a "conformist" stage in the sense that it is acutely tuned to the expectations and judgments of significant others and as yet does not have a sure enough grasp on its own identity and autonomous judgment to construct and maintain an independent perspective. Differences of outlook with others are experienced as differences in "kind" of person. Authority is located in the incumbents of traditional authority roles (if perceived as personally worthy) or in the consensus of a valued, face-to-face group.

Stage 4. Individuative-Reflective faith most appropriately takes form in young adulthood. This stage is marked by a double development. The self, previously sustained in its identity and faith compositions by an interpersonal circle of significant others, now claims an identity no longer defined by the composite of one's roles or meanings to others. Self (identity) and outlook (world view) are differentiated from those of others and become acknowledged factors in the reactions, interpretations and judgments one makes on the actions of self and others. It expresses its intuitions of coherence in an ultimate environment in terms of an explicit system of meanings. Stage 4 typically translates symbols into conceptual meanings. This is a "dymythologizing" stage. It is likely to attend minimally to unconscious factors influencing its judgments and behavior.

Stage 5. Conjunctive faith involves the integration into self and outlook of much that was suppressed or unrecognized in the interest of Stage 4's self-certainty and conscious cognitive and affective adaptation to reality. This stage develops a "second naivete" (Ricoeur) in which symbolic power is reunited with conceptual meanings. Here there must also be a new reclaiming and reworking of one's past. There must be an opening to the voices of one's "deeper self."

Unusual before mid-life, Stage 5 knows the sacrament of defeat and the reality of irrevocable commitments and acts. What the previous stage struggled to clarify, in terms of the boundaries of self and outlook, this stage now makes porous and permeable. Alive to paradox and the truth in apparent contradictions, this stage strives to unify opposites in mind and experience.

Stage 6. Universalizing faith. The transition to Stage 6 involves an overcoming of paradox through a moral and ascetic actualization of the universalizing apprehensions. Heedless of the threats to self, to primary groups, and to the institutional arrangements of the present order that are involved, Stage 6 becomes a disciplined activist incarnation—a making real and tangible—of the imperatives of absolute love and justice of which Stage 5 has partial apprehensions. The self at Stage 6 engages in spending and being spent for the transformation of present reality in the direction of a transcendent actuality.

Stage 6 is exceedingly rare. The persons best described by it have generated faith compositions in which their felt sense of an ultimate environment is inclusive of all being.[15]

It is interesting to note that while Erikson's theory of psychosocial development forms the general background for Fowler's work and was, in fact, the first developmental theory to influence Fowler, Erikson's stages are not now considered to be aspects of faith development. The influence of Erikson's theory is still prominent, however, especially in the later stages of Fowler's work.

In reflecting on what his theory has contributed thus far, Fowler notes that faith development theory provides, first of all, a language to discuss the development of faith. This language is not reductionistic. This language is non-pathological. Rather, it deals with the normal development of the human person. The language of faith development is suitable also for a religious and pluralistic context. It suits the secular world as well as the religious world. Fowler believes too that his contribution lies in focusing on the role of faith in human development, and he believes that he has operationalized faith in terms which can be researched.

Fowler is not blind to, in fact he is quite aware of, the many problems which still need to be addressed by his theory. Of particular concern is the relationship between the operational structures and the contents of faith. The theory itself does not intend to separate structure from context, community and content; but does want to be able to investigate the structures of thinking. Fowler believes that perhaps he has neglected the structuring power of the contents of faith. When we embrace certain contents such as centers of value, images of power, and master stories which we tell ourselves in order to be able to interpret and respond to the events of our life, then we embrace, perhaps implicitly, a structure of some sort. Thus, the need arises to investigate further the relationship between structure and content. The new structural features of the successive stages mean that the contents of the previous faith stage are reworked in a new context, but what is the influence of radical changes in the contents of faith? Do these lead to or flow from structural changes? It is issues such as these which need to be further pursued.

The study of faith development also needs to investigate the relationship of the psychology of adult development to faith. Fowler has begun to investigate this area in some of his recent work and he notes the parallels between his work and that of Levinson and other theorists of adult development. He offers a dynamic model which seeks to incorporate the varied elements which influence adult development, but this model is more descriptive than empirically verified.[16] It points out many elements which influence and go into the dynamics of faith development in adults. These include the unconscious, which is another area where Fowler sees that his theory needs further elaboration. What precisely is the relationship between unconscious factors and adult development?

Finally, Fowler believes that he needs to address the relationship of his stage theory to a normative vision of adult growth. What, in fact, is or should be the norm of adult growth and in what sense can stage six be seen to be normative?

It is important to realize that Fowler's work, despite its ten-year history, is really incipient. It is in need, as Fowler realizes, of a great deal of further investigation. The empirical foundation, while impressive in its breadth, is not firmly established. A great deal of work still needs to be accomplished in order to show the validity and reliability of the data obtained. The methodology of the faith development interviews which Fowler and his associates have used needs to be more fully elaborated and given more precision if the faith development data is to be seen as having validity. As Fowler himself indicates, the cross-cultural validity of his work still needs to be confirmed. This suggestive theory, then, remains in an initial state. A great deal of further investigation will have to be undertaken if this theory is to be put on a firmer foundation.

Critical Comments

Recently there has been some critical commentary on Fowler's work. This commentary in itself seems rather initial and reflects the beginning of critical assessment of Fowler's book. These comments in general do not invalidate the theory of faith development, but they do raise serious questions for further consideration.

Initially, some question can and should be raised about the empirical validity of Fowler's work. Even Fowler himself notes, "...tests of statistical significance and other indices of the reliability of the sample have not yet been undertaken."[17] A close analysis of the available data indicates that a great deal of work remains to be done in this area.[18] Similarly, it should be noted that further work needs to be done on the interview itself. That is, one needs to deal more specifically with the total communication taking place in the interview. The emphasis now on verbal response needs to be complemented by analysis of non-verbal communication.[19]

Other elements of this theory also bear examination. The precise definition of faith needs to be examined closely. Craig Dykstra contends that there are two definitions of faith in the theory. The first, the structural one, seems predominant in the early stages, while the second, involving vision and centers of value and power, dominates in the later stages.[20] There is also concern expressed by some authors regarding the Eriksonian basis for the theory. The compatibility of the work of Erikson and the work of the structuralists, Piaget and Kohlberg, is questionable. There is a need for more elaboration of the foundation of this theory.[21] A further very significant question along these lines is in regard to the precise nature of the stages. As Paul Philibert cogently asks, what precisely are these stages of? It is hard to see how the structures of one stage lead to the structures of the following stage.[22] A question arises here as to whether these are seven highly correlated aspects peculiar to this culture and very intuitively persuasive, or whether they are, in fact, structural stages in the Piagetian sense. Fowler contends that these are truly structural stages, but, in fact, the evidence is not overwhelmingly convincing.

Questions are also raised about the normativeness of Fowler's work. These questions concern the precise way in which the stage theory can serve as a norm for judging a person's development in faith.[23] In this regard there is some questioning of the two highest stages in Fowler's system. Gabriel Moran questions the existence of stage six and believes that stage six responses, as Fowler cites them, are really merely examples of stage five.[24]

Finally, the problem of distinguishing content from structure continues to bedevil the work on stages of faith. Fowler, of course, realizes the problem but it continues to perdure. Moran notes that Fowler in his work *Stages of Faith* brings the content, the Kingdom of God, into his sixth stage. Moran argues that this image is not sufficient, but rather needs to be complemented by other important images, such as incarnation, salvation, resurrection, etc. Furthermore, while the religious meaning of faith comes more to the fore in Fowler's stages five and six, this raises the question whether a religious element cannot be seen to be present earlier.[25]

These comments are not intended to gainsay the significant work that Fowler has accomplished but to indicate the need for ongoing development. Much remains to be done with this system.

Concluding Reflections

The detailed examination of the justice theory of Lawrence Kohlberg and the faith development work of James Fowler presents an exciting, stimulating new area of concern in virtue theory. The precise contribution of developmental work to Christian reflection remains to be delineated. It is interesting to note the questions that the structural-developmental approaches, which we have briefly surveyed, stimulate. For example, what precisely is the relationship of justice and faith? Here we see that justice is part of the "faithing" proposed by Fowler. This in some ways shows a basic interrelationship of virtues. The relationship, however, remains to be explored. The contribution of the empirical investigations of developmentalists to our thinking about virtue could be quite substantial. The task remains to integrate this work as it progresses into the substantial body of critical Christian reflection on the theological and moral virtues. The Fowlerian emphasis on faith needs to be coordinated with the traditional emphasis on love as central to Christian life. Present-day methods of empirical investigation could and should be quite helpful in delineating a renewed virtue theory. Critical investigation of the virtues of contemporary Christians may be helpful in articulating a theology of the virtues and their interrelationships. A great deal, then, remains to be done in this vibrant and exciting area of investigation.

5
The Future Task of
Virtue Theory

The foregoing chapters, which discuss in some detail contemporary thinking on virtue, point to the relevance of this renewed interest in virtue thinking. While the authors cited may not be in the majority among contemporary ethicists, they do constitute a significant number of important thinkers. There is an important ecumenical dimension to their thought as well, in that both Catholic and Protestant theologians are involved in reflecting on virtue. Their task, however, is incipient at best. That is, just as traditional theories cannot be accepted *carte blanche* because of the difference between previous cultures and our own, so contemporary virtue theory needs to continue to be rethought in light of present-day history and present-day society. Thus, the main task of virtue theory seems to still lie in the future. There is a need to construct a contemporary theology of virtue which is broad in its scope and compelling in its explanatory power.

Any such attempt at integration will have to consider the significant findings of developmental psychology. The developmental psychology of adulthood is just in its infancy. The findings of Levinson *et al* have already been mentioned above. The significant investigations of Carol

Gilligan and her associates at Harvard remain to be integrated into contemporary adult developmental psychology. These findings are tentative at best, as they are based on a limited number of studies. They indicate, however, that developmental psychology will have to make certain major shifts in its conception of the development of the person to full adult maturity. Gilligan has investigated the adult development of women, and her initial findings indicate that there is some variation in patterns of male and female development.[1] Gilligan's findings and speculations do not necessarily negate the work of Levinson and others. For instance, the work of Wendy Ann Stewart[2] lends some general support to Levinson's findings, though not in every particular. It would appear that it will be quite some time before the newer findings on the adult development of women are fully integrated into the existing data on adult development of men. A complete overview of adult growth is something that will not be with us immediately but most probably will take a number of years to work out. Yet there is a need, despite the state of flux of the data, to incorporate an awareness of these development theories into one's reflections on the theology of virtue. Not to do so would weaken the relevance of contemporary reflection on virtue to the situation of the person of today.

In attempting to absorb this data into one's thinking about virtue, it seems important to adopt a critical attitude. Such an attitude would take into account the descriptive nature of such data and its limits in getting to reality or in proving anything. The fact that there are various schools of thought in psychology raises a point of caution. There is also a great deal of ferment going on in psychology today. As is indicated in occasional articles in *The American Psychologist,* psychologists themselves are seeking for ways to unify the disparate data coming in from the various branches and schools of thought in psychology.

A further point which needs to be raised is that developmental models need a great deal of refinement. First of all, there is some problem with getting at what remains the same in development. Contemporary personality theory indicates that personality often does not change much after college age. Yet developmentalists stress that change seems to occur throughout life. There is need for a great deal more precision in indicating what it is that develops, and what it is that stays the same, as one goes through the life cycle. It is important to note here, too, that the most problematic areas of Kohlberg's and Fowler's stage theories are precisely those stages which occur in adulthood. Similarly, the works of Levinson and Gilligan are just beginning to give a cogent explanation of adult development. Thus, it is important to understand that these investigations, while very informative and helpful, need to be seen as limited and as not encompassing all of reality. Some further issues also need to be addressed such as the development of those who do not follow the ordinary course and, more precisely, what is the role of regression. Implicit here is the fact that life events seem to play a major role in a person's coming to maturity, and these life events vary, not just according to the "cohort" which one is in (that is, the particular generation and its common experiences), but also according to the unique events which influence each individual's growth and development. These few questions indicate some of the strengths and weaknesses of developmental theory.

We see, then, that there are some important developmental models which may be useful in constructing a theology of virtue. Yet their present initial state and the significant questions that can be raised in regard to them make one cautious in basing one's reflections on virtue entirely on their findings.

Additional critical reflection also seems called for in a related area, that of narrative theology. Writers such as

108 *The Future Task of Virtue Theory*

McIntyre and Hauerwas stress the importance of narrative as giving unity to a theology of virtue. This fits in with the contemporary emphasis on narrative and biography and can be quite integrative because such narratives encompass liturgy, aesthetics and other elements that are important for an overall theological approach. But there seems to be a need for some further study of narrative theology.[3] It seems necessary to incorporate some of the critical and controlling elements from literary theory such as point of view into contemporary discussions of narrative in order to bring more substance and critical awareness to this imaginative but amorphous approach to theologizing.

All of this indicates that, while virtue theory is filled with extensive opportunities and possibilities for growth, there is a need for an ongoing study of the elements that are being proposed for incorporation into the theology of virtue. The breadth of the integrative power of such a theology will call for critical awareness in a number of areas and then for interdisciplinary cooperation.

The Possibilities of an Augustinian/Salesian Approach

The previous remarks on developmental psychology and literary criticism, along with our extensive review of the contemporary thinking on virtue, lead one to propose the possible strength of an Augustinian/Salesian approach to the theology of virtue. St Augustine is well known for his emphasis on love as the central virtue for the Christian.[4] For Augustine, charity is the root of all the virtues. "The point here is that charity, as the one root of the virtues and at the same time, of course, capable of gradual development, produces in varying degrees acts that fall under different virtues."[5] Thus, all the virtues for Augustine, while distinct in some ways, are rooted in, related to, and powered by love.

This central Augustinian thought has been developed in various ways in the Christian tradition. For instance, it finds an important expression in the works of St. Francis de Sales (1567-1622), a bishop and doctor of the Church. St. Francis, following Augustine, sees love as the central virtue and elaborates on the four stages of love which the soul passes through as it grows more deeply in the spiritual life.[6] He further specifies the centrality of love which St. Augustine stresses and provides a more contemporary insight enlivened by the Christian humanism of the Renaissance. His stress, like Augustine's, is on the importance of experience for spiritual growth. This Augustinian/Salesian stress on love as uniting all the virtues fits in well with an emphasis on the existential virtues which was noted earlier in this work. In this system these existential virtues can be transformed by love. Such an approach might also be congenial in many ways to Karl Rahner's stress on the love of God and love of neighbor. Likewise, the developmental virtues as delineated by Meissner and Evans can be seen as leading to the fullness of love and thus as being related in an intrinsic way to the central Christian virtue. So, too, Haring's approach to the eschatological virtues, which are so scriptural in nature, is quite open, it would seem, to being centered on this central Christian virtue so evident in Scripture. The stage approach characteristic of Salesian spiritual theology, which in some ways seems akin to that of Erikson, would also seem intriguingly open to further elaboration in dialogue with contemporary developmental theory.

In conclusion, I would like to suggest that an emphasis on the Augustinian/Salesian heritage which comes out of the Catholic tradition provides a fruitful way of approaching the contemporary discussion of virtue. Such an approach remains to be systematically developed, of course, but it does seem to allow a number of contemporary emphases to shine through very clearly and to have a significant number of parallels to the varied elements that would need to be incorporated into a contemporary developmental theory.

Concluding Reflections

The foregoing chapters affirm that virtue thinking is a very active and creative area in contemporary theology. It will continue to make a large and growing contribution to moral and ethical discussions. Of course, it needs a great deal more work,[7] and this work will probably continue over an extended period of time. The area, however, is very fertile and promises a great deal of fruitfulness in an ongoing way. Perhaps even the contemporary Catholic impasse on moral norms will be affected by this renaissance in virtue thinking. Certainly the virtue tradition, seemingly moribund a few decades ago, is now experiencing a revival which will be with us for years to come.

Notes

Introduction

1. Jacques M. Pohier, "Psychology and Virtue," *New Black-friars* 50 (1969): 483.
2. San Antonio: Trinity University Press, 1975.
3. See, for example, John P. Langan, "Augustine on the Unity and Interconnection of the Virtues," *Harvard Theological Review* 72 (1979): 81–95 and William C. Spohn, S.J., "Sovereign Beauty: Jonathan Edwards and the Nature of True Virtue," *Theological Studies* 42 (1981): 394-421.
4. Notre Dame: University of Notre Dame Press, 1981.
5. Ibid., p. 57.
6. Ibid., p. 140.
7. *The Seasons of a Man's Life* (New York: Ballantine Books, 1978). See also George Vaillant, *Adaptation to Life* (Boston: Little, Brown and Company, 1977).
8. Gail Sheehy, *Passages* (New York: E.P. Dutton, 1976); *Pathfinders* (New York: William Morrow and Co., 1981).
9. This will be discussed more at length below.
10. See Richard A. McCormick, S.J., "Notes on Moral Theology: 1980," *Theological Studies* 42 (1981): 90–100.
11. See Tom L. Beauchamp and James F. Childress, *Principles of Biomedical Ethics,* 2nd ed. (New York: Oxford University Press, 1983): pp. 255–80.

12. Karl Hermann Schelkle, *Theology of the New Testament,* Vol. 1: *Morality,* English version by William A. Jurgens (Collegeville: The Liturgical Press, 1973), p. 207.

13. *Dictionnaire de Theologie Catholique,* s.v. "Vertu," by A. Michel.

14. See *Theological Dictionary of the New Testament,* s.v. "arete" by Otto Bauernfeind; Schelkle, p. 209.

15. Schelkle, p. 210.

16. See Elisabeth Schussler Fiorenza, "Discipleship and Patriarchy: Early Christian Ethos and Christian Ethics in a Feminist Theological Perspective," *Annual of the Society of Christian Ethics* (1982): 141. Fiorenza argues from a feminist perspective that these lists represent the unsatisfactory endpoint of a New Testament trajectory which began with the equality in the Spirit evident in the early community and concluded with an accommodation to the patriarchal order evident in these lists of duties. See pp. 138–155 of the article just cited.

17. Evelyn Eaton Whitehead and James D. Whitehead, *Christian Life Patterns* (Garden City: Doubleday and Co., 1979), pp. 14–18, 39–40.

Chapter 1
Virtue in Contemporary Catholic Thought

1. Josef Pieper, *The Four Cardinal Virtues* (Notre Dame: University of Notre Dame Press, 1966). This work originally appeared as separate essays in German and English between 1954 and 1959.

2. Gilbert Meilaender, "Josef Pieper: Explorations in the Thoughts of a Philosopher of Virtue," *Journal of Religious Ethics* 11 (1983): 116.

3. Pieper, p. 9.

4. Ibid., p. 44.

5. Ibid., p. 51.

6. Ibid., p. 129.

7. Ibid., p. 151. *"Studiositas, Curiositas*—by these are meant temperateness and intemperance, respectively, in the natural

striving for knowledge: above all, in the indulgence of the sensual perception of the manifold sensuous beauty of the world..." (p. 198).

8. See Meilander, pp. 117–121, for a discussion of the unity of the virtues in Pieper's work.

9. Meilander, p. 129.

10. Romano Guardini, *The Virtues: On Forms of Moral Life*, trans. Stella Lange (Chicago: Henry Regnery, 1967), p. 2.

11. Ibid., p. 16.

12. Ibid., p. 19.

13. Ibid., p. 24.

14. For a good discussion see Louis Roberts, *The Achievement of Karl Rahner* (New York: Herder and Herder, 1967), pp. 134–148.

15. *Sacramentum Mundi*, s.v. "Virtue," by Karl Rahner, p. 337.

16. Karl Rahner, "On the Theology of Hope," in *Theological Investigations*, vol. X, trans. David Bourke (New York: Herder and Herder, 1973), p. 250.

17. See also Karl Rahner, *Foundations of Christian Faith*, trans. William V. Dych (New York: Seabury Press, 1978), pp. 404–405.

18. *Sacramentum Mundi*, p. 340.

19. See *Foundations of Christian Faith*, pp. 398–400.

20. *Sacramentum Mundi*, p. 346.

21. Karl Rahner, "The Unity of Love of God and Love of Neighbor," *Theology Digest* 15 (1967): 89.

22. See also *Foundations of Christian Faith*, pp. 309–310.

23. Bernard Haring, *Free and Faithful in Christ*, vol. 1: *General Moral Theology* (New York: Seabury Press, 1978), p. 168.

24. Ibid., p. 197.

25. Haring develops his ideas on faith at length in vol. 2: *The Truth Will Set You Free* (New York: Seabury Press, 1979), pp. 205–239. Here, for example, he contends that "The more faith is experienced and lived as an undeserved gift of God and as our own free response, the more religious liberty, liberty of conscience and liberty of all people will be promoted. It is through faith that the fundamental option reaches its highest level of consciousness,

freedom and strength... and the highest form of responsibility and co-responsibility flows from the authentic obedience of faith" (p. 216).

26. Haring discusses love at great length in volume 2, pp. 419-491. Haring believes that "The liberating truth of the divine love and our vocation to share in it are present in all parts of a Christian ethics. Here, our theme is one of reflection on the heart of the matter, on the architectural centre of the whole of Christian life" (p. 420).

27. See vol. 3: *Light to the World* (New York: Crossroad, 1981), pp. 235-236.

28. Ibid., vol. 1, p. 202.

29. Ibid., p. 205. For a discussion of hope in greater detail, see vol. 2, pp. 379-418.

30. See the recent Church documents presented by Joseph Gremillion in *The Gospel of Peace and Justice: Catholic Social Teaching Since Pope John* (Maryknoll, N.Y.: Orbis, 1976).

31. Gremillion, p. 514.

32. Charles M. Murphy, "Action for Justice as Constitutive of the Preaching of the Gospel: What Did the 1971 Synod Mean?" *Theological Studies* 44 (1983): 308.

33. See for example Daniel C. Maguire, "The Primacy of Justice in Moral Theology," *Horizons* 10/1 (1983): 77-78; Dale Vree, "On Christian Self-Indulgence," *New Oxford Review* 50/6 (1983): 18.

34. Maguire, p. 84.

35. Vree, p. 18.

36. Maryknoll, N.Y.: Orbis, 1973.

37. Henri J.M. Nouwen, "We Drink From Our Own Wells," *America*, October 15, 1983, p. 207.

38. For a brief summary see Arthur Jones, "Liberation Theology: First World Response to Industrial Capitalism," *National Catholic Reporter*, October 7, 1983, pp. 6-7.

Chapter 2
Christian Character in Contemporary Protestant Ethics

1. Jurgen Moltmann, *Theology of Hope*, trans. James W. Leitch (New York: Harper and Row, 1967).
2. For some background to Moltmann's early work see Francis P. Fiorenza, "Dialectical Theology and Hope," *Heythrop Journal* 9 (1968): 143–163, 384–399 and 10 (1969): 26–42, and George Hunsinger, "The Crucified God and the Political Theology of Violence: A Critical Survey of Jurgen Moltmann's Recent Thought," *Heythrop Journal* 14 (1973): 266–277, 379–395.
3. Jurgen Moltmann, *The Experiment Hope*, ed., trans. with a Foreword by M. Douglas Meeks (Philadelphia: Fortress Press, 1975), p. 45.
4. Ibid., p. 41.
5. Jurgen Moltmann, *Experiences of God,* trans. Margaret Kohl (Philadelphia: Fortress Press, 1980), p. 28.
6. M. Douglas Meeks, *Origins of the Theology of Hope* (Philadelphia: Fortress Press, 1974), p. 8.
7. John J. O'Donnell, *Trinity and Temporality: The Christian Doctrine of God in the Light of Process Theology and the Theology of Hope* (Oxford: Oxford University Press, 1983), p. 139.
8. Chicago: University of Chicago Press, 1968.
9. Ibid., p. 248.
10. Ibid., p. 263. James Laney in his article "Characterization and Moral Judgments" amplifies what Gustafson mentions here. Laney argues that no adequate ethic can neglect feeling and emotion. These need to be reflected upon by rational analysis but even more they need a reflection "... which occurs through a process of characterization of moral life in all its shades and recesses." An advantage of Gustafson's system is that it has a substantial place for the feelings and emotions. *Journal of Religion* 55 (1975): 414.
11. James Gustafson, "Christian Style of Life: Problematics of a Good Idea," in *Christian Ethics and the Community* (Philadelphia: Pilgrim Press, 1971), p. 181.

12. For an interesting essay which bears on many of the points in this brief discussion here and which further clarifies Gustafson's position, see James Gustafson, "Moral Discernment in the Christian Life," which is reprinted in his *Theology and Christian Ethics* (Philadelphia: Pilgrim Press, 1974), pp. 99–119.

13. Stanley Hauerwas, *Character and the Christian Life* (San Antonio: Trinity University Press, 1975), p. 35.

14. Ibid., p. 83.

15. Stanley Hauerwas, *Vision and Virtue: Essays in Christian Ethical Reflection* (Notre Dame: Fides/Claretian, 1974), p. 36.

16. Ibid., p. 2.

17. While vision and character are obviously closely related in Hauerwas' thought, we must agree with Gene Outka that vision's "...precise relation to 'character' is complex and never ...elucidated adequately by Hauerwas." "Character, Vision, and Narrative," *Religious Studies Review* 6 (1980): 114.

18. See for example William K. Frankena, "Conversations with Carney and Hauerwas," *Journal of Religious Ethics* 3 (1975): 45–62; Stanley Hauerwas, "Obligation and Virtue Once More," *Journal of Religious Ethics* 3 (1975): 27–47; and J. Wesley Robbins, "Professor Frankena on Distinguishing an Ethic of Virtue from an Ethic of Duty," *Journal of Religious Ethics* 4 (1976): 57–62. For a good bibliography see David Schenck, Jr., "Recasting the Ethics of Virtue/Ethics of Duty Debate," *Journal of Religious Ethics* 4 (1976): 269–286.

19. Hauerwas, *Character and the Christian Life*, p. 16.

20. Ibid., p. 11.

21. Hauerwas here cites Robert Johann who contends that "A moral act is first of all and in its essence an act of *self-determination*, i.e. an act in which the agent, beyond merely exhibiting the dispositions he has acquired through past activity, newly ratifies or modifies them, and so determines the sort of agent he is to be in the future." Johann, like Hauerwas, would put the stress more on the agent than on the act though both obviously are interrelated. "A Matter of Character," *America* 116 (1967), p. 95.

22. Hauerwas, *Vision and Virtue*, p. 55.

23. Ibid., p. 56.
24. Stanley Hauerwas, with Richard Bondi and David B. Burrell, *Truthfulness and Tragedy: Further Investigations in Christian Ethics* (Notre Dame: University of Notre Dame Press, 1977), p. 8.
25. Stanley Hauerwas, "The Demands of Truthful Story: Ethics and the Pastoral Task," *Chicago Studies* 21/1 (1982): 63.
26. Stanley Hauerwas, *The Peaceable Kingdom: A Primer in Christian Ethics* (Notre Dame: University of Notre Dame Press, 1983), p. xxv.
27. *Truthfulness and Tragedy*, p. 76.
28. Stanley Hauerwas, *A Community of Character: Toward a Constructive Christian Social Ethic* (Notre Dame: University of Notre Dame Press, 1981), p. 136.
29. *Vision and Virtue*, p. 74; see *The Peaceable Kingdom*, pp. 28–29.
30. *A Community of Character*, p. 149.
31. Thomas W. Ogletree, "Stanley Hauerwas, *Character and the Christian Life: A Study in Theological Ethics; Vision and Virtue: Essays in Christian Ethical Reflection;* and with Richard Bondi and David B. Burrell, *Truthfulness and Tragedy: Further Investigations into Christian Ethics,*" *Religious Studies Review* 6 (1980): 25–30.
32. Outka, p. 114.
33. *The Peaceable Kingdom*, p. 40.
34. Ibid., p. 43.
35. See William C. Spohn, review of *A Community of Character,* by Stanley Hauerwas, in *America,* May 29, 1982, pp. 424–425; Richard A. McCormick, "Notes on Moral Theology: 1980," *Theological Studies* 42 (1981): 99; Richard A. McCormick, "Notes on Moral Theology: 1982," *Theological Studies* 44 (1983): 93. Hauerwas' further reflections can be found in *The Peaceable Kingdom,* pp. 59–64.
36. James Childress, "Scripture and Christian Ethics," *Interpretation* 34 (1980): 371–380.
37. McCormick, "Notes on Moral Theology: 1980," p. 95.
38. See the interesting position taken by Tom L. Beauchamp and James F. Childress in their *Principles of Biomedical Ethics,* 2nd ed. (New York: Oxford University Press, 1983), pp. 255–280.

39. New York: Paulist, 1981.
40. See below, Chapter 4.
41. *Vision and Character,* p. 28.
42. Ibid., p. 44.
43. Ibid., p. 59.
44. Ibid., p. 61.
45. Ibid., p. 67.
46. Ibid., p. 95.
47. Ibid., p. 124.
48. Dykstra's strong critique of Kohlberg stands in contrast to the more ameliorative and integrative efforts of other authors. See for example Dykstra's essay, "What Are People Like? An Alternative to Kohlberg's View," in *Moral Development Foundations: Judeo-Christian Alternatives to Piaget/Kohlberg,* ed. Donald M. Joy (Nashville: Abingdon Press, 1983), pp. 153–162. This essay stands in contrast to those of the other contributors.

Chapter 3
Developmental Approaches — Virtue and the Life Cycle

1. 2nd. ed. (Chicago: University of Chicago Press, 1970). Kuhn's book has produced a great deal of critical reaction since its initial appearance in 1962. For some interesting critical analyses of Kuhn's work see Dudley Shapere, "The Paradigm Concept," *Science* 172 (May 1971): 706–709 and Ian Barbour, *Myths, Models and Paradigms* (New York: Harper and Row, 1974).
2. Allan R. Buss, "The Emerging Field of the Sociology of Psychological Knowledge," *American Psychologist* 30 (1975): 988–1002.
3. Norma Haan, "Can Research on Morality Be 'Scientific'?" *American Psychologist* 37 (1982): 1096–1104.
4. Robert A. Segal, "Assessing Social—Scientific Theories of Religion," *The Council on the Study of Religion Bulletin* 13 (1982): 71. See also Thomas A. Russman, "Foundations for Unity and Pluralism," *Communio* 7 (1980): 320–333; Hugo Meynell, "Where the Philosophy of Science Should Go From here," *The Heythrop Journal* 22 (1982): 123–138.

5. Robert M. Doran, S.J. "Jungian Psychology and Christian Spirituality: III," *Review for Religious* 38 (1979): 857-866. Doran explores the relationship of Jungian psychology and Christian spirituality in a series of three articles in *Review for Religious* 38 (1979): 497-510 and 742-752.

6. James Gustafson, *Theology and Christian Ethics* (Philadelphia: Pilgrim Press, 1974), p. 226.

7. Charles E. Curran, *Catholic Moral Theology in Dialogue* (Notre Dame: Fides, 1971; reprinted, University of Notre Dame Press, 1976), p. 20.

8. See Mary L. Restelli, "Distinguishing Features of Secular versus Christian Psychology," *Spiritual Life* 29 (1983): 103-108.

9. Paul J. Philibert, "Moral Education and the Formation of Conscience," in *Principles of Catholic Moral Life*, ed. William E. May (Chicago: Franciscan Herald Press, 1980) pp. 388-389.

10. Curran, pp. 78-80.

11. Paul J. Philibert, "Theological Guidance for Moral Development Research," in *Essays in Morality and Ethics*, ed. James Gaffney (New York: Paulist, 1980), p. 110.

12. A similar point of view is expressed by John M. McDonagh in *Christian Psychology: Toward a New Synthesis* (New York: Crossroad, 1982), p. 107.

13. Erik H. Erikson, *Toys and Reasons* (New York: W.W. Norton and Co., 1977), p. 41.

14. Erik H. Erikson, *Insight and Responsibility* (New York: W.W. Norton and Co., 1964), p. 10.

15. Erik H. Erikson, *The Life Cycle Completed: A Review* (New York: W.W. Norton and Co., 1982), pp. 25-26.

16. Erikson H. Erikson, "Identity and the Life Cycle," *Psychological Issues* 1 (1959): 53.

17. Erik H. Erikson, *Dimensions of a New Identity* (New York: W.W. Norton and Co., 1974), pp. 92-93.

18. *The Life Cycle Completed,* pp. 56-57.

19. Erik H. Erikson, *Childhood and Society,* 2nd ed. revised and enlarged (New York: W.W. Norton and Co., 1963), p. 271.

20. Ibid., p. 250.

21. "Identity and the Life Cycle," p. 109.

22. *Childhood and Society*, p. 263.

23. Erik H. Erikson, *Young Man Luther: A Study in Psycho-analysis and History* (New York: W.W. Norton and Co., 1958), p. 261.

24. *Insight and Responsibility,* p. 113.

25. Ibid., p. 115.

26. Erik H. Erikson, "Reflections on Dr. Borg's Life Cycle," in *Adulthood* ed. Erik H. Erikson (New York, W.W. Norton and Co., 1978), p. 26.

27. *Insight and Responsbility,* p. 119.

28. Ibid., p. 122.

29. Ibid., p. 124.

30. "Reflections on Dr. Borg's Life Cycle," p. 28.

31. *Insight and Responsibility,* p. 127.

32. Ibid., p. 131.

33. Ibid., p. 123.

34. See Daniel Levinson *et al., The Seasons of a Man's Life* (New York: Ballantine Books, 1978); see George Vaillant, *Adaptation to Life* (Boston: Little, Brown and Company, 1977); James Fowler, *Stages of Faith* (San Francisco: Harper and Row, 1981).

35. William W. Meissner, S.J., *Foundations for a Psychology of Grace* (Glen Rock: Paulist Press, 1966), p. 6.

36. William W. Meissner, S.J., "Prolegomena to a Psychology of Grace," *Journal of Religion and Health* 3 (1963-64): 213.

37. "It will become clear that Erikson's contributions come as close as anything in psychological thought to what we have been calling a psychology of grace." Meissner, *Foundations,* p. 153.

38. Meissner, "Prolegomena," p. 225. For a very interesting development of his ideas on faith which shows the impact of Erikson's thinking, see W.W. Meissner, S.J., "Notes on the Psychology of Faith," *Journal of Religion and Health* 8 (1969): 47–75.

39. Meissner, "Prolegomena," p. 229.

40. Donald Evans, *Struggle and Fulfillment: The Inner Dynamics of Religion and Morality* (Cleveland: Collins, 1979), pp. 6–7.

41. Ibid., p. 5.

42. Ibid., p. 120.

43. Ibid., p. 7.

44. Ibid., p. 168.
45. Ibid., p. 163.
46. Stanley Hauerwas and Richard Bondi, "Language, Experience and the Life Well-Lived: A Review of the Work of Donald Evans," *Religious Studies Review* 9 (January 1983): 37.
47. Evelyn Eaton Whitehead and James D. Whitehead, *Christian Life Patterns: The Psychological Challenges and Religious Invitations of Adult Life* (Garden City: Doubleday and Co., 1979), p. 21.
48. Ibid., p. 42.
49. Ibid., p. 59.

Chapter 4
Structural-Developmental Approaches

1. Lawrence Kohlberg, *Essays on Moral Development,* vol. 1: *The Philosophy of Moral Development* (San Francisco: Harper and Row, 1981), pp. 409–412.
2. Lawrence Kohlberg, "Stages of Moral Development as a Basis for Moral Education," in *Moral Development, Moral Education, and Kohlberg,* ed. Brenda Munsey (Birmingham: Religious Education Press, 1980), p. 42.
3. Lawrence Kohlberg, "From Is to Ought," in *Cognitive Development and Epistemology*, ed. T. Mischel (New York: Academic Press, 1971), p. 221.
4. Ibid., p. 195.
5. Paul J. Philibert, "Lawrence Kohlberg's Use of Virtue," *International Philosophical Quarterly* 15 (1975): 455–479.
6. For example, Roger A. Page, "Longitudinal Evidence for the Sequentiality of Kohlberg's Stages of Moral Judgment in Adolescent Males," *Journal of Genetic Psychology* 139/1 (1981): 3–9; George G. Bear and Herbert C. Richards, "Moral Reasoning and Conduct Problems in the Classroom," *Journal of Educational Psychology* 73/5 (1981): 664–670.
7. Lawrence Kohlberg, "Educating for a Just Society: An Updated and Revised Statement," in *Moral Development, Moral*

Education and Kohlberg, ed. Brenda Munsey (Birmingham: Religious Education Press, 1981): 457.

8. Don Locke, "Doing What Comes Morally: The Relation Between Behavior and Stages of Moral Reasoning," *Human Development* 26 (1983): 12.

9. See for example Bernard Rosen, "Kohlberg and the Supposed Mutual Support of Ethical and Psychological Theory," *Journal for the Theory of Social Behavior* 10/3 (1980): 195–210; Elizabeth L. Simpson, "Moral Development Research: A Case Study of Scientific Cultural Bias," *Human Development* 17 (1974): 82–83.

10. See the essays in *Moral Development Foundations,* ed. Donald M. Joy (Nashville: Abingdon Press, 1983).

11. "Justice and Beyond in Moral Education," *Andover Newton Quarterly* 19/3 (1979): 145, as cited by Paul J. Philibert in "The Motors of Morality: Religion and Relation," in *Moral Development Foundations,* ed. Donald M. Joy (Nashville: Abingdon Press, 1983), p. 86.

12. Minneapolis: Winston Press, 1983.

13. James Fowler, *Stages of Faith* (San Francisco: Harper and Row, 1981), p. 25.

14. Ibid., pp. 244–245.

15. Ibid., pp. 121, 133, 149, 172–173, 182, 197–198, 200.

16. James Fowler, "Stages of Faith and Adults' Life Cycle," in *Faith Development in the Adult Life Cycle,* ed. Kenneth Stokes (New York: W.H. Sadlier, 1982), pp. 178–207.

17. *Stages of Faith,* p. 313.

18. See also Alfred McBride, "Response to Fowler: Fears about Procedure," in *Values and Moral Development,* ed. Thomas C. Hennesey (New York: Paulist Press, 1976); Margaret Gorman, review of *Stages of Faith,* by James W. Fowler, in *Horizons* 9/1 (1982): 110.

19. Dr. Carl Schneider, "The Hermeneutics of Suspicion and Retrieval: Psychodynamic and Faith Development Theories," Paper presented at the Institute of Faith Development Studies, Atlanta, June 30, 1982.

20. Craig Dykstra, "Christian Education and Faith Development Theory," paper presented at the Institute of Faith Development Studies, Atlanta, June 29, 1982; see also Moran, pp. 123–125.

21. See Moran, p. 110.

22. Paul J. Philibert, review of *Stages of Faith*, by James W. Fowler, in *Horizons* 9/1 (1982): 120.

23. Ibid., p. 121; Moran, p. 113.

24. Moran, pp. 118–119.

25. Moran, pp. 122–123.

Chapter 5
The Future Task of Virtue Theory

1. Carol Gilligan, *In a Different Voice* (Cambridge: Harvard University Press, 1982).

2. Wendy A. Stewart, "The Formation of the Early Adult Life Structure in Women" (Ph.D. Dissertation, Columbia University, 1977).

3. See, for example, some of the questions raised by John D. Barbour in "Religious Resentment and Public Virtues," *Journal of Religious Ethics* 11 (Fall 1983): 264–279.

4. See John P. Langan, "Augustine on the Unity and Interconnection of the Virtues," *Harvard Theological Review* 72 (1979): 81–95.

5. Ibid., p. 92.

6. St. Francis de Sales, *Treatise on the Love of God*, translated with an introduction and notes by John K. Ryan (Rockford: Tan Books, 1974), vol. II, pp. 149–152.

7. John Boyle, "Seminar on Moral Theology. A. Rethinking Virtue," *Proceedings of the Catholic Theological Society of America* 38 (1983): 117–118.

Selected Bibliography

Beauchamp, Tom L. and Childress, James F. *Principles of Biomedical Ethics*. 2nd ed. New York: Oxford University Press, 1983.

Buss, Allan R. "The Emerging Field of the Sociology of Psychological Knowledge." *American Psychologist* 30 (1975): 988-1002.

Childress, James. "Scripture and Christian Ethics." *Interpretation* 34 (1980): 371-80.

Curran, Charles E. *Catholic Moral Theology in Dialogue*. Notre Dame: Fides, 1972; reprint ed., University of Notre Dame Press, 1976.

Dictionnaire de Theologie Catholique. s.v. "Vertu," by A. Michel.

Doran, Robert M., S.J. "Jungian Psychology and Christian Spirituality." *Review for Religious* 38 (1979): 497-510, 742-52, 857-66.

Dykstra, Craig. *Vision and Character*. New York: Paulist, 1981.

Erikson, Erik H. *Young Man Luther: A Study in Psychoanalysis and History*. New York: W.W. Norton and Co., 1958.

____. "Identity and the Life Cycle." *Psychological Issues* 1 (1959): 1-171.

____ *Childhood and Society*. 2nd ed. New York: W.W. Norton and Co., 1963.

____. *Insight and Responsibility*. New York: W.W. Norton and Co., 1964.

____. *Dimensions of a New Identity*. New York: W.W. Norton and Co., 1974.

____. *Toys and Reasons*. New York: W.W. Norton and Co., 1977.

____. "Reflections on Dr. Borg's Life Cycle." In *Adulthood*, pp. 1-31. Edited by Erik H. Erikson. New York: W.W. Norton and Co., 1978.

____. *The Life Cycle Completed: A Review*. New York: W.W. Norton and Co., 1982.

Evans, Donald. *Struggle and Fulfillment: The Inner Dynamics of Religion and Morality.* Cleveland: William Collins Publishing Company, 1979.

Fiorenza, Elisabeth Schussler. "Discipleship and Patriarchy: Early Christian Ethos and Christian Ethics in a Feminist Theological Perspective." *Annual of the Society of Christian Ethics* (1982): 131–172.

Fowler, James. *Stages of Faith: The Psychology of Human Development and the Quest for Meaning.* San Francisco: Harper and Row, 1981.

____. "Stages of Faith and Adults' Life Cycle." In *Faith Development in the Adult Life Cycle,* pp. 178–207. Edited by Kenneth Stokes. New York: W.H. Sadlier, 1982.

Gilligan, Carol. *In a Different Voice.* Cambridge: Harvard University Press, 1982.

The Gospel of Peace and Justice: Catholic Social Teaching Since Pope John. Presented by Joseph Gremillion. Maryknoll: Orbis, 1976.

Guardini, Romano. *The Virtues: On Forms of Moral Life.* Translated by Stella Lange. Chicago: Henry Regnery Co., 1967.

Gustafson, James. *Christ and the Moral Life.* Chicago: University of Chicago Press, 1968.

____. *Christian Ethics and the Community.* Philadelphia: Pilgrim Press, 1971.

____. *Theology and Christian Ethics.* Philadelphia: Pilgrim Press, 1974.

Gutierrez, Gustavo. *A Theology of Liberation.* Maryknoll: Orbis, 1973.

Haan, Norma. "Can Research on Morality Be 'Scientific'?" *American Psychologist* 37 (1982): 1096–1104.

Haring, Bernard. *Free and Faithful in Christ.* 3 vols. New York: Seabury Press, 1978, 1979; New York: Crossroad, 1981.

Hauerwas, Stanley. *Vision and Virtue.* Notre Dame: Fides/Claretian, 1974.

____. *Character and the Christian Life: A Study in Theological Ethics.* San Antonio: Trinity University Press, 1975.

____. *The Peaceable Kingdom: A Primer in Christian Ethics.* Notre Dame: University of Notre Dame Press, 1983.

Hauerwas, Stanley and Bondi, Richard. "Language, Experience and the Life Well-Lived: A Review of the Work of Donald Evans." *Religious Studies Review* 9 (January 1983): 33–41.

Hauerwas, Stanley, Bondi, Richard, and Burrell, David B. *Truthfulness and Tragedy: Further Investigations in Christian Ethics.* Notre Dame: University of Notre Dame Press, 1977.

Jones, Arthur. "Liberation Theology: First World Response to Industrial Capitalism." *National Catholic Reporter* 7 October 1983, pp. 6–7.

Kohlberg, Lawrence. "Educating for a Just Society: An Updated and Revised Statement." In *Moral Development, Moral Education, and Kohlberg*, pp. 455–70. Edited by Brenda Munsey. Birmingham: Religious Education Press, 1980.

———. *Essays on Moral Development.* Vol. 1: *The Philosophy of Moral Development.* San Francisco: Harper and Row, 1981.

———. "From Is to Ought." In *Cognitive Development and Epistemology*, pp. 151–235. Edited by T. Mischel. New York: Academic Press, 1971.

———. "Stages of Moral Development as a Basis for Moral Education." In *Moral Development, Moral Education, and Kohlberg*, pp. 15–98. Edited by Brenda Munsey, Birmingham: Religious Education Press, 1980.

Kuhn, Thomas. *The Structure of Scientific Revolutions.* 2nd ed. Chicago: University of Chicago Press, 1970.

Levinson, Daniel J., Darrow, C.N., Klein, E.B., Levinson, M.H., and McKee, B. *The Seasons of a Man's Life.* New York: Ballantine Books, 1978.

Locke, Don. "Doing What Comes Morally: The Relation Between Behavior and Stages of Moral Reasoning." *Human Development* 26 (1983): 11–25.

MacIntyre, Alasdair. *After Virtue.* Notre Dame: University of Notre Dame Press, 1981.

McCormick, Richard A., S.J. "Notes on Moral Theology: 1980." *Theological Studies* 42 (1981): 90–100.

Maguire, Daniel C. "The Primacy of Justice in Moral Theology." *Horizons* 10/1 (1983): 72-85.

Meeks, M. Douglas, *Origins of the Theology of Hope,* Philadelphia: Fortress Press, 1974.

Meilaender, Gilbert. "Josef Pieper: Explorations in the Thoughts of a Philosopher of Virtue." *Journal of Religious Ethics* 11 (1983): 114–34.

Meissner, William. *Foundations for a Psychology of Grace.* New York: Paulist Press, 1966.

Moltmann, Jurgen. *Experiences of God.* Translated by Margaret Kohl. Philadelphia: Fortress Press, 1980.

———. *The Experiment Hope.* Edited, translated and with a foreword by M. Douglas Meeks. Philadelphia: Fortress Press, 1975.

———. *Theology of Hope.* Translated by James W. Leitch. New York: Harper and Row, 1967.

Moral Development Foundations. Edited by Donald M. Joy. Nashville: Abingdon Press, 1983.

Moran, Gabriel. *Religious Education Development.* Minneapolis: Winston Press, 1983.

Murphy, Charles M. "Action for Justice as Constitutive of the Preaching of the Gospel: What Did the 1971 Synod Mean?" *Theological Studies* 44 (1983): 298–311.

Nouwen, Henri J.M. "We Drink From Our Own Wells." *America* 15 October 1983, pp. 205–08.

O'Donnell, John J. *Trinity and Temporality: The Christian Doctrine of God in the Light of Process Theology and the Theology of Hope.* Oxford: Oxford University Press, 1983.

Ogletree, Thomas W. "Stanley Hauerwas, *Character and the Christian Life: A Study in Theological Ethics; Vision and Virtue: Essays in Christian Ethical Reflection;* and with Richard Bondi and David B. Burrell, *Truthfulness and Tragedy: Further Investigations into Christian Ethics. Religious Studies Review* 6 (1980): 25–30.

Outka, Gene. "Character, Vision, and Narrative." *Religious Studies Review* 6 (1980) 110–118.

Philibert, Paul J. "Lawrence Kohlberg's Use of Virtue." *International Philosophical Quarterly* 15 (1975): 455–79.

———. "Moral Education and the Formation of Conscience." In *Principles of Catholic Moral Life,* pp. 383–411. Edited by William E. May. Chicago: Franciscan Herald Press, 1980.

———"Theological Guidance for Moral Development Research."

In *Essays in Morality and Ethics*, pp. 106–125. Edited by James Gaffney. New York: Paulist Press, 1980.

———. Review of *Stages of Faith* by James W. Fowler. *Horizons* 9/1 (1982): 118–22.

Pieper, Josef. *The Four Cardinal Virtues*. Notre Dame: University of Notre Dame Press, 1966.

Pohier, Jacques M. "Psychology and Virtue." *New Blackfriars* 50 (1969): 483–90.

Rahner, Karl. *Foundations of Christian Faith*. Translated by William V. Dych. New York: Seabury Press, 1978.

———. "The Unity of Love of God and Love of Neighbor." *Theology Digest* 15 (1967): 87–93.

———. "On the Theology of Hope." In *Theological Investigations*. Vol. X, pp. 242–259. Translated by David Bourke. New York: Herder and Herder, 1973.

Sacramentum Mundi. s.v. "Virtue," by Karl Rahner.

Sales, St. Francis de. *Treatise on the Love of God*. Translated with an introduction and notes by John K. Ryan. Rockford: Tan Books, 1974.

Schelkle, Karl Hermann. *Theology of the New Testament*. Vol. 1: *Morality*. English version by William A. Jurgens. Collegeville: The Liturgical Press, 1973.

Schenck, David, Jr. "Recasting the 'Ethics of Virtue/Ethics of Duty' Debate." *Journal of Religious Ethics* 4 (1976): 269–86.

Segal, Robert A. "Assessing Social-Scientific Theories of Religion." *The Council on the Study of Religion Bulletin* 13 (1982): 69–72.

Sheehy, Gail. *Passages*. New York: E.P. Dutton, 1976.

———. *Pathfinders*. New York: William Morrow and Co., 1981.

Stewart, Wendy Ann. "The Formation of the Early Adult Life Structure in Women." Ph.D. dissertation, Columbia University, 1977.

Theological Dictionary of the New Testament. s.v. "arete" by Otto Bauernfeind.

Vree, Dale. "On Christian Self-Indulgence." *New Oxford Review* 50/6 (1983): 8–20.

Whitehead, Evelyn Eaton and Whitehead, James D. *Christian Life Patterns*. Garden City: Doubleday, 1979.